DISC

W9-DEA-368

TWENTIETH-CENTURY
WORLD HISTORY
A SELECT BIBLIOGRAPHY

TWENTIETH-CENTURY WORLD HISTORY
A SELECT BIBLIOGRAPHY

FREDA HARCOURT and FRANCIS ROBINSON

CROOM HELM LONDON

BARNES & NOBLE BOOKS · NEW YORK
(a division of Harper & Row Publishers, Inc.)

Z
6204
H 363
1979

© 1979 Freda Harcourt and Francis Robinson
Croom Helm Ltd, 2-10 St John's Road, London SW11

British Library Cataloguing in Publication Data

Harcourt, Freda
    Twentieth-century world history.
    1. History, Modern — 20th century.
    I   Title   II. Robinson, Francis
    909.82   D421

    ISBN 0-7099-0020-1

Published in the USA 1979 by
Harper & Row Publishers, Inc.
Barnes & Noble Import Division

Library of Congress Cataloging in Publication Data

Harcourt, Freda.
    Twentieth-century world history.

    1. History, Modern — 20th century — Bibliography.
I. Robinson, Francis, joint author.   II. Title.
Z6204.H363   [D421]   909.82   79-10154
ISBN 0-06-492680-X

Printed in Great Britain by
Biddles Ltd, Guildford, Surrey

CONTENTS

INTRODUCTION

World history, and more particularly the study of recent world history, is a new subject. It could be said that it has history on its side, as events increasingly encourage us to view the world in international and even global terms. Certainly it is a subject that ought to be studied. We are likely to be better historians for learning about the world outside Europe and North America; we are better historians too for encountering areas where the writing of history has been so richly informed by the insights of sociology, anthropology and political science.

Since 1973 a course entitled *World History since the end of the nineteenth century* has been taught as part of the BA degree in History in the University of London. The course itself was the product of lengthy discussions among experts in many different fields in the London School of History, and when the course was launched it represented a consensus of views about shape and content. One of the guiding principles on which there was general agreement was that the paper should avoid the detailed subject matter which forms the substance of established courses in the degree; another, that the aim of world history as a discipline should be to try to develop an informed conceptual approach to movements, ideologies and processes which have been world-wide in their influence and impact in the twentieth century; and yet another principle was that on a more pragmatic level there should be a framework of the most important developments within and between states and regions, and that the study of these concrete events should balance the study of concepts. Since teaching began, the course has benefited from the experience of those taking part, all of whom have contributed a great deal within their own fields of interest and expert knowledge. But teachers have been very conscious of the fact that the course ought to be tailored to its student consumers. It has become apparent, precisely because of the World History course's great range and inter-disciplinary approach, that more substantial guidance is desirable if it is to be followed by the uninitiated with profit and understanding.

The idea of a comprehensive bibliography, intended to help both students and teachers, owes its inspiration to Professor R.F. Leslie of Queen Mary College, who was one of the founding fathers of the course. At the outset of the enterprise, now three or four years ago, teachers in several disciplines were invited to offer advice or book titles. Many did so then, many have done so more recently, and a substantial collection of titles was gathered together.

All the help so willingly offered by our colleagues we gladly and gratefully acknowledge. But a bibliography, especially one designed to chart the unfamiliar depths of world history, has to have shape and form as well as content if it is to be useful. We took it upon ourselves to complete the task of ordering and filling out the lists that had been accumulated. We also felt strongly that the bibliography would serve its purpose best if its structure gave a more precise definition to the subject matter of the course. We have therefore devised a series of headings, 27 in all, some of a thematic and some of a pragmatic nature, which in general fall within the more loosely constructed guidelines originally laid down. This is not to say that we wish to put forward a rigid 'syllabus'. The School of History rightly abhors the kind of structure which ties a subject down too firmly: history, more than most disciplines, constantly changes its perspective and thrives on flexibility. We should not like to give the impression that we think world history consists only of the subjects of our 27 headings. But we are convinced that a new, challenging and somewhat unformed course of study can, at this stage of its development, only benefit from greater definition and from a more coherent frame of reference.

There were certain constraints which we had to take into account. First, and most obvious, several courses in the BA and associated degrees provide, in isolation, as it were, for the detailed study of Europe, Africa, the Americas and Asia and of many of the countries and regions in these continents. Thus, while we have deliberately excluded the specific history of areas covered by other papers, we have made a point of including those topics and themes of world-wide significance. Nor have we set out to make experts of our students. The World History paper is one among many taken for the degree, and it was always intended to be general rather than particular because specialised studies are undertaken in other parts of the degree course. Rather our object has been to provide the material for stimulating the interest and encouraging the inter-disciplinary reading which we hope will promote a deeper appreciation of subjects of global importance in the present century.

The world history we have outlined in our bibliography is to a large extent Third World history, Europe and North America being covered only in so far as they affect the world beyond their shores. One of the functions of the study of world history is to correct the Eurocentric and North American bias evident in much history teaching. It is for this reason that we have adopted the neutral term West Asia to describe the area known to the western world as the Middle East. After all, the primacy of the societies bordering the North Atlantic basin is brief when measured against the long history of our planet. But we also believe that the history of Third World societies, their interaction with each other and with Europe and North America is a viable entity for study and an effective frame in which the processes common to many societies in the twentieth century may be examined.

The bibliography also sets out to indicate the problems which students will be encouraged to study. We consider this to be an important part of the exercise of definition. It may, indeed, sharpen the controversies about what should and what should not be included in the course. But if students are not to flounder in a subject of such immense historiographical range and depth, some shape ought to be given to its broadly accepted limits. It need hardly be said that the problems we have identified are to a considerable extent the product of the collective wisdom of those involved in developing and teaching the subject in the university. But the exact shape of the bibliography, and the final decisions about both sections and titles, are our responsibility alone.

The 27 headings into which the bibliography is divided are intended to direct attention to the areas and problems we think important. Sections 1-18 are thematic, that is, they are common to most societies in the twentieth century. Sections 19-27 focus on developments within major areas of the world or on developments in their relations with one another. We have laid special emphasis on themes because one of the advantages of the daunting range of the course is the opportunity it offers for fruitful comparison of processes in different societies. But students should beware of regarding the study of themes as distinct from studies of specific areas. They will discover that the concepts they are invited to explore in the themes are of considerable value when they approach the more detailed problems associated with specific areas. Equally the detailed knowledge won in studying problems in a particular context should provide the firm platform from which the themes can be approached with confidence.

Each of the 27 sections is introduced by a brief outline of what it involves and what its main problems are, and by a short commentary on the literature to furnish a skeleton guide. The bibliography which follows is not intended to be comprehensive or definitive. It recommends those books which we believe to be valuable, although there are certainly others which will be useful. The lists of books under each

heading have usually been divided into three sections. The first consists
of a few works of an introductory nature; the second groups titles which
make a general contribution in terms of ideas or subject matter; and in
the third section are works, often monographs, on more limited areas
or on particular aspects of the problem under review. The decision to
place a book in one section rather than another has not been based on
an estimate of its intrinsic worth but on the contribution it has to
make to the subject. Books in all three sections should therefore be
treated as equally important on the understanding that there is a logical
sequence to the order in which titles are grouped. Students will be
unlikely to appreciate the more detailed works until some of the
preliminary reading has been done.

We acknowledge the advice given on particular sections by B. Bond,
J.G. Grahl, Ray Hall, R.F. Leslie, P. Preston, G.N. Sanderson, D. Sassoon
and A. Stockwell; and our thanks are due to Mrs Carol Toms for typing
a difficult manuscript cheerfully and efficiently.

F.H., Queen Mary College
F.R., Royal Holloway College
University of London
October, 1978

There are no introductions to the subject with a really satisfactory range and penetration. Major's book offers the best short general introduction, while Barraclough is a useful thematic treatment. Worsley, an anthropologist, looks particularly at the world outside Europe and North America. Black views the subject from the angle of social and political science and contains a stimulating short essay. Kenwood & Lougheed give an outline of the international economy. Watt *et al.* is useful for a straightforward account of international relations.

No student of this subject should be without a good historical atlas. Finding one, however, is not so easy. The *Penguin Atlas* has the merit of being cheap and readily available, but the disadvantages of relatively few maps, cluttered presentation, and of having been written for a German audience. Boyd's *Atlas*, on the other hand, presents information with clarity and intelligence but tends to concentrate on 'trouble spots'. By far the best atlas is the *New Cambridge Modern History Atlas* which is available in paperback. It covers a much longer period than the twentieth century, but most students, we imagine, would be grateful for an atlas which served them well in other periods too. *The Times Atlas of World History* has a section on the twentieth century, which, in line with its general approach, avoids a Eurocentric focus. It is likely to be a classic.

G. Barraclough | *An Introduction to Contemporary History* (Penguin Books, Harmondsworth, 1967 / Gannon, Santa Fé, NM, 1968)

C.E. Black | *The Dynamics of Modernization: a study in comparative history* (Harper & Row, New York, 1967)

A.G. Kenwood & A.L. Lougheed | *The Growth of the International Economy 1820-1960: an introductory text* (Allen & Unwin, London, 1971)

J. Major

The Contemporary World: a historical introduction (Methuen, London, 1970)

D.C. Watt, F. Spencer & N. Brown

A History of the World in the Twentieth Century (Hodder & Stoughton, London, 1967 / Morrow, New York, 1968)

P. Worsley

The Third World (Weidenfeld & Nicolson, London, 2nd edn, 1967 / University of Chicago Press, Chicago, 2nd edn, 1970)

* * * *

G. Barraclough (ed.)

The Times Atlas of World History (Times Books, London, 1978)

A.K.H. Boyd

An Atlas of World Affairs (Methuen, London, 6th edn, 1970)

H.C. Darby & H. Fullard (eds.)

The New Cambridge Modern History Atlas (Cambridge University Press, Cambridge, 1970)

H. Kinder & W. Hilgeman (eds.)

The Penguin Atlas of World History vol. II (Penguin Books, Harmondsworth, 1978)

R.I. Moore (ed.)

The Hamlyn Historical Atlas (Hamlyn, London, forthcoming)

1   THE BASIS OF POWER

Wealth in trade and resources forms the basis of world power, but problems of poverty have become an important preoccupation of the later twentieth century: glaring inequalities between rich and poor could lead to political instability and conflict. The nineteenth-century network of world trade based on London ended with the First World War and was replaced, after an interval of uncertainty marked by the catastrophic crisis of capitalism in the 1930s, by the American dollar as the pivot of world trade, a role befitting the overwhelming strength of the American economy. Aid as a political weapon in the rivalry between the super-powers has been one facet of the post-1945 world; multinational companies, wielding immense influence throughout the world, are another. Ideological differences notwithstanding, the underlying trend has been towards greater integration in the realms of international trade.

Landes, from a long historical perspective, reaches the twentieth century in the last three chapters; though European in orientation, this splendid account of what makes up the intricate process of industrialisation is suggestive of the difficulty of repeating the pattern at great speed in the Third World. Ashworth, brief and necessarily superficial, should be supplemented by Kenwood & Lougheed for a more up-to-date outline. Shonfield is interesting on the post-war period, with an important emphasis on the shift from private to public resources. Weil & Davidson is good for the way the international economy works, while Rolfe & Burtle looks critically at the international monetary system. Tugendhat provides an introductory account of the multinationals and should be read with Turner, both books being interesting and informative. Penrose is a work of scholarship by a distinguished specialist. Economic aid is dealt with from different angles by Black and Goldman. White is outstanding on the politics of foreign aid and should be read in conjunction with Hayter who writes very critically on this subject. As authorities on developing economies, both Myint and Myrdal deserve attention. Bairoch has much useful information on Third World economies. Kindleberger (*World in Depression*) is essential reading on the slump of the 1930s, while in his *Power and Politics* the close links between politics and economics are discussed, a theme also covered in Baldwin.

W. Ashworth	*A Short History of the International Economy 1850-1950* (Longmans Green, London, New York, 1952)
A. Harrison	*The Framework of International Activity: the international economy and the rise of the state in the twentieth century* (Macmillan, London, 1967 / St. Martin's Press, New York, 1967)
A.G. Kenwood & A.L. Lougheed	*The Growth of the International Economy: an introductory text* (Allen & Unwin, London, 1971)
D.S. Landes	*The Unbound Prometheus: technological change and industrial development in western Europe from 1750 to the present* (Cambridge University Press, Cambridge, 1969)

* * * *

T. Hayter	*Aid as Imperialism* (Penguin Books, Harmondsworth, 1971)
C.P. Kindleberger	*Power and Money: the economics of international politics and the politics of international economics* (Basic Books, New York, 1970)
C.P. Kindleberger	*The World in Depression 1929-1939* (Allen Lane, London, 1973 / University of California Press, Berkeley, 1973)
S.E. Rolfe & J.L. Burtle	*The Great Wheel: the world monetary system: a reinterpretation* (Quandrangle, New York, 1973 / Macmillan, London, 1974)
A. Shonfield	*Modern Capitalism: the changing balance of public and private power* (Oxford University Press, London, New York, 1966)

C. Tugendhat | *The Multinationals* (Penguin Books, Harmondsworth, 1971)

L. Turner | *Invisible Empires: multinational companies and the modern world* (Hamilton, London, 1970 / Harcourt Brace Jovanovich, New York, 1971)

L. Turner | *Multinational Companies and the Third World* (Allen Lane, London, 1973 / Hill & Wang, New York, 1973)

G.L. Weil & I. Davidson | *The Gold War: the story of the world's monetary crisis* (Secker & Warburg, London, 1970 / Holt, Rinehart & Winston, New York, 1970)

J.A. White | *The Politics of Foreign Aid* (Bodley Head, London, 1974 / St. Martin's Press, New York, 1974)

* * * *

P. Bairoch (tr. C. Postan) | *The Economic Development of the Third World Since 1900* (Methuen, London, 1975 / University of California Press, Berkeley, 1975)

D.A. Baldwin | *Economic Development and American Foreign Policy 1943 to 1962* (Chicago University Press, Chicago, 1966)

L.D. Black | *The Strategy of Foreign Aid* (Van Nostrand, Princeton, 1968)

M.I. Goldman | *Soviet Foreign Aid* (Praeger, New York, 1967)

R.S. Jordan (ed.) | *Multinational Cooperation: economic, social and scientific development* (Oxford University Press, London, New York, 1972)

H. Myint   *The Economics of Developing Countries*
                            (Hutchinson, London, 4th edn, 1973)

G. Myrdal   *The Challenge of World Poverty: a world
                            anti-poverty programme in outline* (Allen
                            Lane, London, 1970 / Pantheon Books,
                            New York, 1970)

E.T. Penrose   *The Large International Firm in Develop-
                            ing Countries: the international petroleum
                            industry* (Allen & Unwin, London, 1968 /
                            MIT Press, Cambridge, Mass., 1969)

M. Wilkins   *The Maturing of Multinational Enterprise:
                            American business abroad from 1914 to
                            1970* (Harvard University Press, Cambridge,
                            Mass., 1974)

2 NATIONALISM AND NATIONALIST MOVEMENTS

The twentieth century is the age of the nation state. A major process during this period has been, and still is, the emergence of 'new' nations throughout the world. An important subject of historical study has come to be the explanation of how these 'new' nations have been formed. The subject is vast; it bears on most aspects of the workings of human societies. Two sets of problems, in particular, engage historians. The first, and the less important, focuses on ideology. It concerns the growth of nationalist ideologies and their role in the making of nations, though these ideologies have been found in general to be of greater significance inside Europe than outside. The second, and the more important, concentrates on nationalist movements. Historians seek to understand the drives behind the growth and development of nationalist movements. They wish to identify the social groups which take the lead, and to discover how a sense of nationality was communicated, if it was, to the population at large. Then there are problems concerning the choice of national identities. Why should some movements coalesce around language, others around religion and yet others around the state framework created by a colonial power? The study of the subject benefits from the comparison of one nationalist movement with another but it should be remembered that each movement is *sui generis*.

There is no introduction which embraces the subject as a whole. Smith (*Theories of Nationalism*) categorises the various theories surrounding it, and Kedourie (*Nationalism*) provides a handy introduction to the historical development of nationalism as ideology. Seton-Watson and Smith (*Nationalist Movements*) provide first-class introductions to the problems and the vast range of examples associated with nationalist movements. Akzin, Deutsch (*Nationalism and Social Communication*), Gellner and Hertz deal with the formation of nationalism and national consciousness from sociological angles. Brass tackles the fascinating problem of how nationalist movements come to coalesce around one as opposed to another identity: the needs of elites in competition for power, he believes, explains much. Worsley offers a useful introduction to Afro-Asian nationalism and Von der Mehden concentrates on a particular feature of the phenomenon in Asia — the role of religion. Case studies of aspects of nationalism or nationalist movements in specific societies are listed in several titles. Seal demonstrates clearly

19

the role of British imperialism in dictating the form and development of Indian nationalism, while Robinson does the same for the development of Muslim nationalism in India. Haim, Karpat and Binder set out the various ideological strands that go to make Arab nationalism. Duiker explores the relationship between communism and nationalism in Vietnam, and Johnson argues for the existence of peasant nationalism in China, though his findings would run counter to much recent anthropological research. The subject can be followed further in the various area sections of the bibliography.

E. Kedourie   *Nationalism* (Hutchinson, London, 1960 / Praeger, New York, rev. edn, 1961)

H. Seton-Watson   *Nations and States: an enquiry into the origins of nations and the politics of nationalism* (Methuen, London, 1977 / Westview Press, Boulder, Col., 1977)

B.C. Shafer   *Faces of Nationalism: new realities and old myths* (Harcourt Brace Jovanovich, New York, 1972)

A.D. Smith   *Theories of Nationalism* (Duckworth, London, 1971/Harper & Row, New York, 1972)

A.D. Smith (ed.)   *Nationalist Movements* (Macmillan, London, 1976 / St. Martin's Press, New York, 1977)

                           * * * *

B. Akzin   *State[s] and Nation[s]* (Hutchinson, London, 1964 / Doubleday, Garden City, 1966)

P.R. Brass   *Language, Religion and Politics in North India* (Cambridge University Press, Cambridge, 1974)

K.W. Deutsch   *Nationalism and Social Communication: an inquiry into the foundations of nationality* (MIT Press, Cambridge, Mass., 2nd edn, 1966)

R. Emerson — *From Empire to Nation; the rise to self-assertion of Asian and African peoples* (Harvard University Press, Cambridge, Mass., 1960 / Oxford University Press, London, 1970)

E. Gellner — *Thought and Change* (Weidenfeld & Nicolson, London, 1964 / University of Chicago Press, Chicago, 1964)

F.O. Hertz — *Nationality in History and Politics: a psychology and sociology of national sentiment and nationalism* (Routledge & Kegan Paul, London, 1944 / Oxford University Press, New York, 1944)

E. Kamenka (ed.) — *Nationalism: the nature and evolution of an idea* (Edward Arnold, London, 1973)

E. Kedourie (ed.) — *Nationalism in Asia and Africa* (World Pub. Co., New York, 1970 / Weidenfeld & Nicolson, London, 1971)

F.R. Von der Mehden — *Religion and Nationalism in Southeast Asia: Burma, Indonesia, the Philippines* (University of Wisconsin Press, Madison, 1963)

P. Worsley — *The Third World* (Weidenfeld & Nicolson, London, 2nd edn, 1967 / University of Chicago Press, Chicago, 2nd edn, 1970)

* * * *

G. Antonius — *The Arab Awakening: the story of the Arab national movement* (Hamish Hamilton, London, 1938 / Lippincott, Philadelphia, 1939)

L. Binder — *The Ideological Revolution in the Middle East* (John Wiley, New York, 1964)

J.S. Coleman

Nigeria: background to nationalism (University of California Press, Berkeley, 1958 / Cambridge University Press, Cambridge, 1959)

K.W. Deutsch

Nationalism and its Alternatives (Knopf, New York, 1969)

W.J. Duiker

The Rise of Nationalism in Vietnam, 1900-1941 (Cornell University Press, Ithaca, 1976)

S. Haim (ed.)

Arab Nationalism: an anthology (Cambridge University Press, Cambridge, 1962 / University of California Press, Berkeley, 1962)

T. Hodgkin

Nationalism in Colonial Africa (Muller, London, 1956 / New York University Press, New York, 1957)

C.A. Johnson

Peasant Nationalism and Communist Power: the emergence of revolutionary China 1937-1945 (Stanford University Press, Stanford, 1962 / Oxford University Press, London, 1963)

G. McT. Kahin

Nationalism and Revolution in Indonesia (Cornell University Press, Ithaca, 1952 / Oxford University Press, London, 1953)

K.H. Karpat (ed.)

Political and Social Thought in the Contemporary Middle East (Pall Mall, London, 1968 / Praeger, New York, 1968)

D. Kushner

The Rise of Turkish Nationalism 1860-1908 (Frank Cass, London, 1977)

W.Z. Laqueur

A History of Zionism (Weidenfeld & Nicolson, London, 1972 / Holt, Rinehart & Winston, New York, 1972)

J.M. Lonsdale   'Some Origins of Nationalism in East Africa', *Journal of African History, IX, 1* (1968)

F. Robinson   *Separatism among Indian Muslims: the politics of the United Provinces' Muslims 1860-1923* (Cambridge University Press, Cambridge, 1974)

W.R. Roff   *The Origins of Malay Nationalism* (Oxford University Press, London, New York, 1967)

D.A. Rustow   *A World of Nations: the problems of political modernization* (Brookings Inst., Washington, 1967)

A. Seal   'Imperialism and Nationalism in India', *Modern Asian Studies, 7, 3* (1973)

P. Walshe   *The Rise of African Nationalism in South Africa: the African National Congress 1912-1952* (Hurst, London, 1970 / University of California Press, Berkeley, 1971)

A.P. Whitaker &   *Nationalism in Contemporary Latin America* (Collier-Macmillan, London, 1966 / Free Press, New York, 1966)
D.C. Jordan

3 IMPERIALISM

Problems of definition have provoked a number of fruitful discussions about imperialism since Lenin's classic statement was first published in 1916. The object here is to try to discover what imperialism is and why it happens in theory, and then to examine it in practice in its many different forms. A superficial glance at the world up to 1945 might well have given the impression that imperialism meant possession of poorer areas by richer and technologically more advanced states. A closer look will show that, especially since 1945, imperial domination has not been confined to coloured areas on a map which can easily be distinguished. Nor has imperialism been characteristic only of states in the capitalist orbit of the world. Imperialism has many aspects. There are the various techniques of government which were evolved by different imperial powers to suit changing circumstances. Imperial domination was often undertaken for defence or for strategic advantage in great-power rivalry. Sometimes, too, cultural imperialism, transmitted through language and teaching, whether secular or religious, makes an obvious starting-point for the study of this subject. At heart, however, imperialism is best understood in economic terms and it is on this aspect that the bibliography will focus.

Brown is lucid and illuminating about the economics of imperialism and should be regarded as basic reading. Owen & Sutcliffe, in Part I, considers a number of different arguments about definition; in Part II, contemporary imperialism is considered and Part III is devoted to case studies. Horowitz in *Imperialism and Revolution* and in the collection of essays entitled *Containment and Revolution* looks especially at Soviet imperialism. Parkinson and Gerassi both provide basic material on US imperialism in Latin America, a theme further explored in Frank and Furtado, while Andreski presents a sociological analysis of that relationship. Gough Sharma looks at the revolutionary legacy left by formal imperialism in Asia. Gann & Duignan deals in a descriptive way with the imperial experience in Africa, and so does Wilson. These accounts should be measured against the theoretical approaches in Lichtheim and Kiernan. The most recent form of imperialism, foreign aid, finds a vigorous critic in Hayter. The article by Robinson & Gallagher shows that in the nineteenth century, as in the twentieth, possession was not an essential part of imperialism. Moore, in a stimulating synthesis, sheds new light on its social origins.

24

M.B. Brown
The Economics of Imperialism (Penguin Books, Harmondsworth, 1974)

D. Horowitz
Imperialism and Revolution (Allen Lane, London, 1969)

D. Horowitz
Empire and Revolution (Random House, New York, 1969)

V.G. Kiernan
Marxism and Imperialism (E. Arnold, London, 1974 / St. Martin's Press, New York, 1975)

G. Lichtheim
Imperialism (Penguin Books, Harmondsworth, 1971 / Praeger, New York, 1971)

* * * *

S. Andreski
Parasitism and Subversion: the case of Latin America (Weidenfeld & Nicolson, London, 1966 / Pantheon Books, New York, 1967)

N. Bukharin
Imperialism (Merlin Press, London, repr. 1971)

C. Furtado (tr. S. Macedo)
Economic Development of Latin America: a survey from colonial times to the Cuban revolution (Cambridge University Press, Cambridge, 2nd edn, 1976)

J. Gerassi
The Great Fear in Latin America (Collier-Macmillan, London, 1963 / Macmillan, New York, 1963)

K. Gough & R. Sharma (eds.)
Imperialism and Revolution in South Asia (Monthly Review Press, London, New York, 1973)

T. Hayter
Aid as Imperialism (Penguin Books, Harmondsworth, 1971)

D. Horowitz (ed.)   *Containment and Revolution: western policy towards social revolution, 1917 to Vietnam* (Blond, London, 1967 / Beacon Press, Boston, 1967)

V.I. Lenin   *Imperialism, the Highest Stage of Capitalism* (International Publishers, New York, 1963, and in various collections)

F. Parkinson   *Latin America, the Cold War and the World Powers 1945-1973* (Sage, London, Beverly Hills, 1974)

* * * *

A.G. Frank   *Capitalism and Underdevelopment in Latin America: historical studies of Chile and Brazil* (Monthly Review Press, New York, rev. edn, 1969)

L.H. Gann & P. Duignan (eds.)   *Colonialism in Africa 1870-1960, vol. 4, The Economics of Imperialism* (Cambridge University Press, Cambridge, 1975)

B. Moore   *The Social Origins of Dictatorship and Democracy: lord and peasant in the making of the modern world* (Penguin Books, Harmondsworth, 1967 / Beacon Press, Boston, 1969)

R.J. Owen & R.B. Sutcliffe (eds.)   *Studies in the Theory of Imperialism* (Longman, London, New York, 1972)

R. Robinson & J. Gallagher   'The Imperialism of Free Trade', *Economic History Review, Sec. ser., VI, 1* (1953)

H.S. Wilson   *The Imperial Experience in Sub-Saharan Africa Since 1870* (University of Minnesota Press, Minneapolis, 1977 / Oxford University Press, Oxford, 1977)

4 DECOLONISATION

Colonisation means literally the movement of people from one territory to another where they aim to settle. But in terms of recent world history the word colonisation has come to refer to the process by which the European powers, in the main, came to rule the greater part of the world outside Europe. A feature of the twentieth century, particularly since the First World War, has been decolonisation, or the withdrawal of European powers from these areas. Several questions concern the historian. Why did the European powers leave their colonies, and why did some do so amidst bloodshed while others contrived an orderly and even dignified retreat? To what extent were the Europeans pushed and harried out of their colonies and to what extent did they go of their own accord? How important in the process were the colonial nationalist movements, changes in the value of colonies to the mother country, the development of anti-colonialist attitudes in the metropolitan societies, and anti-colonial pressures from the USA, the USSR and the United Nations? What factors influenced the timing of the process? How far were links maintained between colonial power and former colony after independence? And who has gained from institutions such as the Commonwealth?

By far the best introduction is von Albertini's comprehensive study which also benefits from its German author's air of disengagement. Gann & Duignin and Low & Smith deal with decolonisation in British Africa while Gordon and Fanon deal with the important case of French withdrawal from Algeria. Monroe offers a comprehensive and balanced treatment of British withdrawal from West Asia, and Pluvier does the same for the European powers in South-east Asia. Drummond demonstrates the limited value of the empire to Britain between the two world wars while Tomlinson's excellent first chapter shows that during this period India was becoming a burden on the British taxpayer. Robb, Moore, Hodson and Menon illustrate the processes at work, largely constitutional ones, in the most important example of decolonisation, that of India, while Low is concerned to emphasise its significance for the later withdrawal from Africa. Louis sets out the anti-colonial role of the USA, Boersner that of Bolshevik Russia, and El-Ayouty demonstrates the use made by the Afro-Asian bloc of the United Nations as an anti-colonial platform. McIntyre offers a simple introduction to the transition from colonies to Commonwealth. Mehrotra explains how the Commonwealth concept was expanded to absorb the non-white colonies, and how Indians were reconciled to membership. Miller examines the functioning of the Commonwealth in the 1950s and 1960s.

R. von Albertini
(tr. F. Garvie)
Decolonization: the administration and future of the colonies, 1919-1960 (Doubleday, Garden City, 1971)

H. Grimal (tr. S. De Vos)
Decolonization: the British, French, Dutch and Belgian empires, 1919-1963 (Routledge & Kegan Paul, London, 1978 / Westview Press, Boulder, Col., 1978)

* * * *

Y. El-Ayouty
The United Nations and Decolonization: the role of Afro-Asia (Martinus Nijhoff, The Hague, 1971)

G. Bolton
Britain's Legacy Overseas (Oxford University Press, London, New York, 1973)

R. Emerson
From Empire to Nation: the rise to self-assertion of Asian and African peoples (Harvard University Press, Cambridge, Mass., 1960)

L.H. Gann & P. Duignan
Colonialism in Africa 1870-1960, vol. 2, The History and Politics of Colonialism 1914-1960 (Cambridge University Press, Cambridge, 1970)

W.R. Louis
Imperialism at Bay (Clarendon Press, Oxford, 1977)

D.A. Low
Lion Rampant: essays in the study of British imperialism (Cass, London, 1973)

E. Monroe
Britain's moment in the Middle East 1914-1956 (Chatto & Windus, London,

1963 / Johns Hopkins Press, Baltimore, 1963)

J. Pluvier   *South-East Asia from Colonialism to Independence* (Oxford University Press, Kuala Lumpur, New York, 1974)

T. Smith   'A Comparative Study of French and British Decolonization', *Comparative Studies in Society and History, 20, 1* (1978)

                            * * * *

D. Boersner   *The Bolsheviks and the National and Colonial Question 1917-1928* (Librairie E. Droz, Geneva, 1957)

I.M. Drummond   *Imperial Economic Policy 1917-1939: studies in expansion and protection* (Allen & Unwin, London, 1974)

F. Fanon   *The Wretched of the Earth* (Grove Press, (tr. C. Farrington)   New York, 1965 / Penguin Books, Harmondsworth, 1967)

D.C. Gordon   *The Passing of French Algeria* (Oxford University Press, London, New York, 1966)

H.D. Hall   *Commonwealth: a history of the British Commonwealth of Nations* (Van Nostrand Reinhold, New York, 1971)

H.V. Hodson   *The Great Divide: Britain, India, Pakistan* (Hutchinson, London, 1969 / Atheneum, New York, 1971)

D.A. Low & A. Smith   *History of East Africa vol. III* (Clarendon (eds.)   Press, Oxford, 1976)

W.D. McIntyre   *Colonies into Commonwealth* (Blandford, London, 1966 / Walker, New York, 1967)

N. Mansergh   *The Commonwealth Experience* (Weidenfeld & Nicolson, London, 1969 /Praeger, New York, 1969)

S.R. Mehrotra   *India and the Commonwealth 1885-1929* (Allen & Unwin, London, 1965 / Praeger, New York, 1965)

V.P. Menon   *The Transfer of Power in India* (Longmans Green, London, 1957 / Princeton University Press, Princeton, 1957)

J.D.B. Miller   *Survey of Commonwealth Affairs: problems of expansion and attrition 1953-1969* (Oxford University Press, London, New York, 1974)

R.J. Moore   *The Crisis of Indian Unity 1917-1940* (Clarendon Press, Oxford, 1974)

M. Perham   *The Colonial Reckoning: the end of imperial rule in Africa in the light of British experience* (Collins, London, 1961 / Knopf, New York, 1962)

P.G. Robb   *The Government of India and Reform: policies towards politics and the constitution 1916-1921* (Oxford University Press, London, 1976)

B.R. Tomlinson   *The Indian National Congress and the Raj, 1929-1942: the penultimate phase* (Macmillan, London, 1976)

5 COMMUNISM

The first aim of this section is to relate the theories of Marx, as enunciated in the context of nineteenth-century Britain, to the reality of the original Communist state in Russia. The influence of the Third International in the inter-war years led to the belief that all future communist states would be based upon the Russian model. Experience since 1945 has shown this to be unfounded. The second aim therefore is to determine how and why the theories have been altered. Even states which had regimes imposed upon them in the aftermath of the war have demonstrated, in time, a remarkable degree of independence, and China followed an entirely different road from Russia. Altogether the second half of the twentieth century has seen the demolition of the idea of a monolithic communism operating throughout the world, and the impetus towards this general development was undoubtedly provided by the end of the Stalin era. Indeed, various kinds of 'nationalist' communisms have evolved to suit changing circumstances. Western communists have also engaged themselves in new theoretical departures, most notably 'Eurocommunism', which were of particular significance as the economic crisis of the late 1960s engulfed the western world in the early 1970s.

The two very brief accounts of Marx and Engels by McLellan provide an easy introduction to these two theorists, who should be followed up in Walker and in Lichtheim (*Marxism*). Hunt sets out the way the theory shows itself in the running of the Soviet government. The International is expertly examined in Borkenau, and more recent developments are analysed in Claudin (*Communist Movement*), a work of fundamental importance. Poppino is an authority on the international movement in Latin America. Gramsci, the best-known Italian theorist, is introduced in Joll and explored more deeply in Cammett. Fejtö is good for the history of the Soviet bloc in Europe, while McInnes considers the 'new wave' of Marxists who have appeared since 1945. Lowenthal looks at world communism in the light of recent developments while Claudin (*Eurocommunism*) evaluates the new thinking in western Europe. For China, where the most significant development of a national communist theory took place, see section 19. Several other regional and local manifestations are presented below. For a useful summary of post-war revolutionary movements of all kinds, Seton-Watson ranges widely and cites a number of examples.

R.N.C. Hunt — *The Theory and Practice of Communism* (Penguin Books, Harmondsworth, 1963)

D. McLellan — *Marx* (Fontana/Collins, London, 1975)

D. McLellan — *Engels* (Fontana/Collins, London, 1975)

A. Walker — *Marx: His Theory and its Context* (Longman, London, New York, 1978)

* * * *

F. Borkenau — *The Communist International* (Faber, London, 1938)

F. Borkenau — *World Communism: a history of the Communist International* (University of Michigan Press, Ann Arbor, 1962)

S. Carillo (trs. N. Green & A.M. Elliot) — *Eurocommunism and the State* (Lawrence & Wishart, London, 1977 / Lawrence Hill, New York, 1978)

F. Claudin (trs. F. MacDonagh & B. Pearce) — *The Communist Movement: from Comintern to Cominform* (Penguin Books, Harmondsworth, 1975 / Monthly Review Press, New York, 1977)

F. Claudin (tr. J. Wakeham) — *Eurocommunism and the State* (New Left Books, London, 1977 / Schocken Books, New York, 1978)

R. Fejtö (tr. D. Weissbort) — *A History of the People's Democracies: Eastern Europe since Stalin* (Penguin Books, Harmondsworth, 1974)

G.F. Hudson — *Fifty Years of Communism: theory and practice 1917-1967* (Watts, London, 1968 / Basic Books, New York, 1968)

C.A. Johnson (ed.) — *Change in Communist Systems* (Stanford University Press, Stanford, 1970)

J. Joll — *Gramsci* (Fontana/Collins, London, 1977)

M.D. Kennedy — *A [Short] History of Communism in Asia* (Weidenfeld & Nicolson, London, 1957 / Praeger, New York, 1957)

G. Lichtheim — *Marxism, an Historical and Critical Study* (Routledge & Kegan Paul, London, 1961 / Praeger, New York, 1961)

R. Lowenthal — *World Communism: the disintegration of a secular faith* (Oxford University Press, New York, 1964)

N. McInnes — *The Western Marxists* (Alcove Press, London, 1972 / Open Court Pub. Co., La Salle, Ill., 1972)

R.E. Poppino — *International Communism in Latin America: a history of the movement 1917-1963* (Free Press of Glencoe, New York, 1964)

H. Seton-Watson — *The Pattern of Communist Revolution: an historical analysis from Lenin to Krushchev* (Methuen, London, 1960 / Praeger, New York, 1960)

* * * *

J. Braunthal — *History of the International* 2 vols. (Nelson, London, 1966 / Praeger, New York, 1967)

J. Cammett — *Antonio Gramsci and the Origins of Italian Communism* (Stanford University Press, Stanford, 1967)

G.S. Harris — *The Origins of Communism in Turkey* (Hoover Inst., Stanford, 1967)

P.J. Honey — *Communism in North Vietnam: its role in the Sino-Soviet dispute* (MIT Press, Cambridge, Mass., 1963)

I.L. Horowitz — *Cuban Communism* (Aldine Pub. Co., Chicago, 1970)

L. Kolakowski — *Main Currents of Marxism* 3 vols. (Oxford University Press, Oxford, 1978)

M. Ram — *Indian Communism: a split within a split* (Vikas, Delhi, 1969)

A. Suarez (tr. J. Carmichael & E. Halperin) — *Cuba: Castroism and Communism 1959-1966* (MIT Press, Cambridge, Mass., 1967)

R. Tiersky — *French Communism 1920-1970* (Columbia University Press, New York, 1974)

F.N. Trager (ed.) — *Marxism in Southeast Asia: a study of four countries* (Stanford University Press, Stanford, 1959)

6 FASCISM

A major difficulty in any discussion of fascism arises out of the problem of definition. Unlike communism which has Marx as a fixed point of reference, fascism has no recognisable ideological base and scholars differ a great deal about what is and what is not a fascist regime. Can fascism occur at any time and at any stage in a society's development? The most recent research would seem to be producing a consensus, namely that fascism occurs in society at a critical point in its process of industrialisation. To determine the kind of society which is, for historical reasons, predisposed towards fascism, and the particular point at which fascism may be said to have manifested itself, is the essence of the problem.

Some writers have approached the subject by describing the forms of fascism which are generally accepted as such and then finding common ground amongst them. Carsten is the leading exponent of this approach. A different exercise is to be found in Kitchen: brief but fundamental, and essential reading for this subject, Kitchen sets out a coherent and readily accessible theory of fascism. Woolf includes several essays which examine different aspects of fascist theory. The two issues of the *Journal of Contemporary History* are devoted to exploring different facets of fascism, and, separated by a decade, show how the search for a satisfactory theory has developed over the years. Moore suggests ways in which different societies react to the kind of tensions likely to make a fascist reaction possible. Mayer (in both works), though difficult to read, repays the effort for the light shed on fascism as a counter-revolutionary movement. De Felice, a great admirer of Mussolini, is interesting on that account but should be read with caution and balanced by Guérin and Vajda.

M. Kitchen	*Fascism* (Macmillan, London, 1976 / Verry, Mystic, Conn., 1977)

* * * *

F. Carsten	*The Rise of Fascism* (Batsford, London, 1967 / University of California Press, Berkeley, 1967)

D. Guérin
(tr. F. & M. Merrill)

Fascism and Big Business (Pathfinder Press, New York, 2nd edn, 1973)

Journal of Contemporary History 1, 1 (1966); *11, 4* (1976)

B. Moore

The Social Origins of Dictatorship and Democracy: lord and peasant in the making of the modern world (Penguin Books, Harmondsworth, 1967 / Beacon Press, Boston, 1969)

M. Vajda

Fascism as a Mass Movement (Allison & Busby, London, 1976 / St. Martin's Press, New York, 1976)

S.J. Woolf (ed.)

The Nature of Fascism (Weidenfeld & Nicolson, London, 1968 / Random House, New York, 1969)

* * * *

R. De Felice
(tr. B.H. Everett)

Interpretation of Fascism (Harvard University Press, Cambridge, Mass., 1977)

A.J. Mayer

Politics and Diplomacy of Peacemaking: containment and counterrevolution at Versailles 1918-1919 (Weidenfeld & Nicolson, London, 1968)

A.J. Mayer

The Dynamics of Counterrevolution in Europe 1870-1956: an analytic framework (Harper & Row, New York, 1971)

7 MODERNISATION AND 'TRADITION'

The role played by 'tradition' in the process of modernisation was a major concern of American social scientists in the 1960s. One school, composed particularly of political scientists, saw 'tradition' and 'modernity' as two opposed states. The process of modernisation involved so-called 'traditional' societies adopting institutions or values of so-called 'modern' societies, and because of an accident of history this generally envisaged Asian and African societies adopting the institutions and values of the West. A second school, in which historians and anthropologists tended to predominate, denied the existence of a rigid dichotomy between 'tradition' and 'modernity', stressing the importance of continuities in the development of different societies and their capacity to adapt new institutions and processes in the light of their own genius. Modernisation did not mean westernisation. Each society was treading its own road forward and that road was dictated to a large extent by its history and by its culture. In recent years the advantage in the debate has come to lie very much with the historians and anthropologists. The literature which bears on the subject is vast. The aim of this section is to do no more than indicate a starting-point. The problem can also be pursued in greater depth in other sections of the bibliography, for instance, those on *Religion and the Modern State* (8) and *Political Development* (12).

Black offers a model for a sharp division between 'tradition' and 'modernity'. The Rudolphs, on the other hand, though basing their argument on India, are concerned to make a major statement about the persistence of traditional features within 'modernity'. The position is sustained by Pye & Verba and by Smith in examining two different aspects of political development. It is taken further by Tambiah who emphasises that 'there are deep-seated continuities in the form of structures and dialectical orientations that have persisted through the period of western impact into the present in all Asian societies.' For him continuities are more significant than transformation. This theme is borne out particularly in work on Asian societies. It is stressed by Fairbank, Reischauer & Craig, and it is a point which tends to be dramatically emphasised in the case of Japan. Here Nakane's slim but telling analysis of the persistence of Japanese social organisation from rice cultivation to manufacturing industry is particularly worthy of note. This development in the Japanese context is to be compared with the way in which India's caste system has responded to modernisation (Rudolphs, Srinivas, Kothari). Osborne highlights the significance of traditional forms of resistance in South-east Asia, and Bill & Leiden the persistence of traditional forms of government and political behaviour in several West Asian societies. The monumental volumes in the *Sources of Tradition* series are also valuable.

C.E. Black   *The Dynamics of Modernization: a study in comparative history* (Harper & Row, New York, 1967)

L.W. Pye & S. Verba   *Political Culture and Political Development* (Princeton University Press, Princeton, 1965)

L.I. & S.H. Rudolph   *The Modernity of Tradition: political development in India* (University of Chicago Press, Chicago, 1967)

K.H. Silvert (ed.)   *Churches and States: the religious institution and modernization* (American Universities Field Staff, New York, 1967)

D.E. Smith   *Religion and Political Development* (Little, Brown, Boston, 1970)

S.J. Tambiah   *World Conqueror and World Renouncer: a study of Buddhism and polity in Thailand against a historical background* (Cambridge University Press, Cambridge, 1976)

* * * *

W.T. de Bary (ed.)   *Sources of Japanese Tradition* (Columbia University Press, New York, 1958)

W.T. de Bary (ed.)   *Sources of Indian Tradition* (Columbia University Press, New York, 1958)

W.T. de Bary (ed.)   *Sources of Chinese Tradition* (Columbia

University Press, New York, 1960)

J.A. Bill & C. Leiden — *The Middle East: politics and power* (Allyn & Bacon, Boston, 1974)

H.-D. Evers (ed.) — *Modernization in South-East Asia* (Oxford University Press, New York, 1973)

J.K. Fairbank, E.O. Reischauer & A.M. Craig — *East Asia: the modern transformation* (Houghton Mifflin, Boston, 1965)

E.B. Harvey (ed.) — *Perspectives on Modernization: essays in memory of Ian Weinberg* (University of Toronto Press, Toronto, 1972)

M.B. Jansen (ed.) — *Changing Japanese Attitudes towards Modernization* (Princeton University Press, Princeton, 1965)

R. Kothari (ed.) — *Caste in Indian Politics* (Orient Longman, New Delhi, 1970)

C. Nakane — *Japanese Society* (Penguin Books, Harmondsworth, 1973)

M.E. Osborne — *Region of Revolt: focus on Southeast Asia* (Penguin Books, Harmondsworth, 1971)

D.H. Shively (ed.) — *Tradition and Modernization in Japanese Culture* (Princeton University Press, Princeton, 1971)

M.N. Srinivas — *Caste in Modern India and other Essays* (Asia Publishing House, Bombay, 1962)

8 RELIGION AND THE MODERN STATE

A major feature of the relationship between 'tradition' and 'modernisation' is the interaction between the great religious traditions of the
world, for instance Hinduism, Buddhism, Christianity, Islam, and the
modern state. In the countries of Europe and North America a considerable division between Church and State has been recognised for
many years. But in most societies of Asia, Latin America and, to a
lesser extent Africa, the connections between religious traditions and
the developing modern state have been close in the twentieth century,
and still remain so. One set of problems centres on the relationship
between religion and political authority. In the nineteenth century
there were many societies in which the ruler was either a god or an agent
of God, and the ideological basis of the state was provided entirely by
religious ideas. How have such societies coped with ideas like the
sovereignty of the people, the dissociation of the state from faith, and
the dissociation of law from religion? Another set of problems bears
on the relationship between religion and political behaviour. Most
nationalist movements have been assisted by the use of religious symbols,
religious organisations and religious movements both modernist and
reactionary. Religious factors have also been important in internal
revolts against national governments, for instance the Buddhist revolt
against the Catholic-dominated government of South Vietnam in 1963,
or the conflict between the Muslim Brotherhood and the leaders of the
revolution in Egypt in the 1950s. Then, many societies have political
parties based on religion, while in some religiously plural societies
such parties have led to a demand for the creation of separate national
states, as with the Muslim League in India and its demand for Pakistan. A third set of problems centres on religion and socio-economic
change, a special problem when it is the major function of most Third
World governments to promote and direct fundamental socio-economic
change. Can religions which legitimised the slow-moving socio-economic
structures of 'traditional' societies be reinterpreted to provide ideological support for governments committed to rapid modernisation?
Can the resources of the major religious systems be tapped to legitimise
such changes? Islam which lays down minute rules of social and economic behaviour finds it harder to supply such resources than Buddhism
which does not. Nevertheless, all the great religious traditions have

40

engaged in a fascinating interaction with Marxism, while an excellent example of a religious ideology of social change united to political activism can be found in the Christian Democratic Parties of Latin America.

D.E. Smith's *Sourcebook* provides a good introduction to the major problems in the subject, which would be consolidated by looking at his *Religion and Political Development*. Martin sounds a warning note about drawing too simple a distinction between the religious and the secular. Turning to Christianity, the essays in Landsberger illustrate its role in legitimising and promoting social change in Latin America, while Guzmán's study of Camillo Torres demonstrates how for some this has been taken to the point of participating in revolutionary action. Gibb and W.C. Smith are the best introductions to Islamic responses to modernisation, which for West Asia can be augmented by Hourani, Binder (*Ideological Revolution*) and Karpat. Rosenthal concentrates on specific aspects of the relationship between Islam and the modern state in several countries. Berkes studies Turkey where Islam has been relegated to the private domain, while Binder (*Religion and Politics*) examines the place of Islam in Pakistan, a state which has been based, theoretically at least, on its prescriptions. It is instructive to compare the conflicts which have ensued in Pakistan with those of another state founded on the basis of religion, that of Israel (Marmorstein). The Rudolphs' well-known work contains stimulating essays on the relationship between Hinduism and modern Indian politics, while Derrett is authoritative on the interactions between Hinduism and legislation in India's secular state. D.E. Smith (*Religion and Politics in Burma* and *South Asian Politics and Religion*), Schechter and Von der Mehden are sound on the subject of Buddhism and nationalism and Buddhism and internal revolt. Tambiah's book demonstrates how much political authority in Thailand, and the modern Thai state more generally, owes to the traditional Theravda Buddhist polity. It is a work of the highest class.

D.E. Smith   *Religion and Political Development*
                              (Little, Brown, Boston, 1970)

D.E. Smith (ed.)   *Religion, Politics and Social Change in
                              the Third World: a sourcebook* (Free
                              Press, New York, 1971)

* * * *

R.N. Bellah

Religion and Progress in Modern Asia (Free Press, New York, 1965)

D.A. Martin

The Religious and the Secular: studies in secularization (Routledge & Kegan Paul, London, 1969 / Schocken Books, New York, 1969)

K.H. Silvert (ed.)

Churches and States: the religious institution and modernization (American Universities Field Staff, New York, 1967)

F.R. Von der Mehden

Religion and Nationalism in South-East Asia: Burma, Indonesia, the Philippines (University of Wisconsin Press, Madison, 1965)

* * * *

N. Berkes

The Development of Secularism in Turkey (McGill University Press, Montreal, 1964)

L. Binder

Religion and Politics in Pakistan (Cambridge University Press, Cambridge, 1961 / University of California Press, Berkeley, 1961)

L. Binder

The Ideological Revolution in the Middle East (John Wiley, New York, 1964)

J.D.M. Derrett

Religion, Law and the State in India (Free Press, New York, 1968)

H.A.R. Gibb

Modern Trends in Islam (University of Chicago Press, Chicago, 1947)

G. Guzmán Campos (tr. J.D. Ring)

Camillo Torres (Sheed & Ward, New York, 1969)

A.H. Hourani

Arabic Thought in the Liberal Age, 1798-1939 (Oxford University Press, London, New York, 1962)

K.H. Karpat (ed.)

Political and Social Thought in the Contemporary Middle East (Pall Mall, London, 1968 / Praeger, New York, 1968)

H.A. Landsberger (ed.)

The Church and Social Change in Latin America (University of Notre Dame Press, Notre Dame, 1970)

E. Marmorstein

Heaven at Bay: the Jewish Kulturkampf in the Holy Land (Oxford University Press, London, New York, 1969)

J.L. Mecham

Church and State in Latin America: a history of politico-ecclesiastical relations (University of North Carolina Press, Chapel Hill, rev. edn, 1966)

F.B. Pike

The Conflict Between Church and State in Latin America (Knopf, New York, 1964)

E.I.J. Rosenthal

Islam in the Modern National State (Cambridge University Press, Cambridge, 1965)

L.I. & S.H. Rudolph

The Modernity of Tradition: political development in India (University of Chicago Press, Chicago, 1967)

J. Schechter

The New Face of Buddha: Buddhism and political power in Southeast Asia (Gollancz, London, 1967)

D.E. Smith

Religion and Politics in Burma (Princeton University Press, Princeton, 1965)

D.E. Smith (ed.)

South Asian Politics and Religion (Princeton University Press, Princeton, 1966)

W.C. Smith

Islam in Modern History (Princeton University Press, Princeton, 1957)

S.J. Tambiah   *World Conqueror and World Renouncer:*
                                      a study of Buddhism and polity in Thailand
                                      against a historical background (Cambridge
                                      University Press, Cambridge, 1976)

9 PEASANT SOCIETY AND THE MODERN STATE

More than half the people in the contemporary world are peasants. They form the majority of the population in China, in South-east Asia, in the Indo-Pakistan subcontinent, and in Central and South America. They also form a sizeable minority of the population in east and southern Europe and in West Asia. In a world-wide process over the last 100 years, leaders of modern states have attempted to integrate peasants into the state's economic and political activities. Subsistence farmers, peasants have been forced to play a growing part in the market. Men who have always avoided the representatives of bureaucratic government, they have had to submit to increasing official interference in every aspect of their existence. On the other hand, the fate of many a new state in the world of nations has depended on the capacity of its leaders to understand the peasant societies they govern and to temper their economic and political directives to peasant values. In approaching this subject the historian must, to begin with, be something of an anthropologist and ask: what is a peasant? what are peasant values? what is the nature of peasant society? He needs to have an idea of what persuades a peasant to leave peasant society. How important is contact with another, 'superior', culture? How important is the breakdown of the institutional frameworks on which the peasant has relied down the centuries? The question must be asked: what makes a peasant respond to economic incentives and what makes him participate in organisations which ramify beyond his village. Answers to questions such as these, asked in specific historical contexts, will help to explain both how peasants have come to play major roles in political change in China or Vietnam or Mexico, and how their roles have been less important in India or Indonesia. These answers should also bear on the arguments of those who wish to understand peasant response to the intrusions of the modern state in terms of a simple stratification of society into rich, middle and poor peasantry.

Two readers, Potter and Shanin (*Peasants*), offer good all-round introductions to peasant societies, their economies, their values and their interactions with the modern state. To acquire some 'feel' for peasant society, it is well worth reading one or two specific village studies (Wiser, Stirling, Oscar Lewis, Stein, Eglar), amongst which the Wisers' book is a classic. Lerner suggests that it is culture contact which plays the crucial role in drawing peasants out of peasant society;

Migdal, however, in an important and wide-ranging argument demonstrates that culture contact is not a sufficient cause of why peasants change and that the answer must be found in the breakdown of peasant family and village institutions. The essays in Gough & Sharma, and Frankel's study of the impact of the green revolution, examine the process of economic change and class formation in South Asia, though one suspects that the authors see what they hope to find. Wolf, a non-Marxist, accepts the stratification of peasant society into rich, middle and poor and finds the radical activists amongst the 'socially marginal' middle peasants. Stokes's penetrating essays, instinct with an historian's good sense, challenge the value of viewing the peasantry, in India at least, in class terms at all. Turning to peasant involvement in revolutionary action, Johnson's book should be noted but treated with caution, Race's study lends powerful support to the Migdal thesis, while J.W. Lewis's important collection of essays illustrates what is needed to travel the long path from peasant rebellion to communist revolution. Moore's sweeping study suggests that different relationships between peasant and lord produced different political systems as modern states developed. Bailey examines in miniature the relationship between parliamentary democracy and the older political systems of the Indian village. Finally, it is worth stepping into Europe to look at some of the excellent works on European peasantries interacting with the modern state, for instance, Weber's fine study of this process in nineteenth-century France or Shanin's examination of the confrontation between the leaders of the Russian revolution and their peasant society.

J.M. Potter, M.N. Diaz & G.M. Foster (eds.)	*Peasant Society: a reader* (Little, Brown, Boston, 1967)
T. Shanin (ed.)	*Peasants and Peasant Societies: selected readings* (Penguin Books, Harmondsworth, 1971)

* * * *

L.A. Fallers	*Inequality: social stratification reconsidered* (University of Chicago Press, Chicago, 1973)
G. Hunter	*Modernizing Peasant Societies* (Oxford University Press, London, New York, 1969)

D. Lerner — *The Passing of Traditional Society: modernizing the Middle East* (Free Press, Glencoe, Ill., 1958)

J.W. Lewis (ed.) — *Peasant Rebellions in Communist Asia* (Stanford University Press, Stanford, 1974)

J.S. Migdal — *Peasants, Politics and Revolution: pressures towards political and social change in the third world* (Princeton University Press, Princeton, 1974)

B. Moore — *The Social Origins of Dictatorship and Democracy: lord and peasant in the making of the modern world* (Penguin Books, Harmondsworth, 1967 / Beacon Press, Boston, 1969)

E.R. Wolf — *Peasant Wars of the Twentieth Century* (Harper & Row, New York, 1969 / Faber, London, 1971)

* * * *

F.G. Bailey — *Politics and Social Change: Orissa in 1959* (University of California Press, Berkeley, 1963)

Z.S. Eglar — *A Punjabi Village in Pakistan* (Columbia University Press, New York, 1960)

F.R. Frankel — *India's Green Revolution: economic gains and political costs* (Princeton University Press, Princeton, 1971)

K. Gough & H.P. Sharma — *Imperialism and Revolution in South Asia* (Monthly Review Press, New York, London, 1973)

W. Hinton

Fanshen: a documentary of revolution in a Chinese village (Vintage Books, New York, 1968 / Penguin Books, Harmondsworth, 1972)

E.J. Hobsbawm

Primitive Rebels: studies in archaic forms of social movement in the nineteenth and twentieth centuries (Norton, New York, 1965 / Manchester University Press, 3rd edn, 1971)

C.A. Johnson

Peasant Nationalism and Communist Power: the emergence of revolutionary China 1937-1945 (Stanford University Press, Stanford, 1962)

H.A. Landsberger (ed.)

Latin American Peasant Movements (Cornell University Press, Ithaca, 1969)

O. Lewis

Life in a Mexican Village: Tepoztlan restudied (University of Illinois Press, Urbana, 1963)

A. Pearse

The Latin American Peasant (Cass, London, 1975)

J.F. Petras &
H.Z. Merino (tr. T. Flory)

Peasants in Revolt: a Chilean case study, 1965-1971 (University of Texas Press, Austin, 1972)

J. Race

War Comes to Long An: revolutionary conflict in a Vietnamese province (University of California Press, Berkeley, 1972)

T. Shanin

The Awkward Class: political sociology of peasantry in a developing society; Russia 1910-1925 (Clarendon Press, Oxford, 1972)

W.W. Stein

Hualcan: life in the highlands of Peru (Cornell University Press, Ithaca, 1961)

P. Stirling

Turkish Village (Weidenfeld & Nicolson, London, 1965)

E. Stokes

The Peasant and the Raj: studies in agrarian society and peasant rebellion in colonial India (Cambridge University Press, Cambridge, 1978)

E. Weber

Peasants into Frenchmen: the modernization of rural France 1870-1914 (Stanford University Press, Stanford, 1976 / Chatto & Windus, London, 1977)

W.H. & C.V. Wiser

Behind Mud Walls 1930-1960 (University of California Press, Berkeley, 1971)

10 THE IMPACT OF TECHNOLOGICAL ADVANCE

The twentieth century has witnessed the most rapid technological advances in the history of mankind. In the most obvious way, technology has made the world much more of a unit than it has ever been; this has meant diffusion of knowledge, materials and cultures on an unprecedented scale. And just as space travel has opened up horizons hitherto only dreamed of, developments in destructive weaponry have made mankind vulnerable as never before. It is appropriate to ask how these innovations have affected man, society and therefore the course of history.

Historians have given this important theme less attention than it deserves, most works on technology and society stopping short at 1900. Cardwell is a readable survey for the non-specialist but has only a brief concluding chapter on the present century. Cipolla, in Chapter 6, ranges generally over the social effects of technology on society in the inter-war years. Landes conveys a sense of the dynamic impetus of technological society in the last three chapters which deal with modern times. Braverman is essential reading for an understanding of what technology means in human terms, while Wiener discusses the impact of the computer age on the ordinary citizen. Reid explores the social and moral consequences of new technology in war and peace. Taton is useful for factual information, easily understood, about the advances of the twentieth century in many different fields, including medicine. The essays in Kranzberg & Davenport range over a wide historical spectrum, relating the significance of technology to society.

D.S.L. Cardwell

[Turning Points in Western Technology: a study of] Technology, Science and History (Heinemann, London, 1972 / Science History Publications, New York, 1972)

C.M. Cipolla (ed.)

The Fontana Economic History of Europe: The Twentieth Century, Part One (Collins/ Fontana, London, 1976)

R. Taton
(tr. A.J. Pomerans)

A General History of the Sciences: Science in the Twentieth Century (Thames & Hudson, London, 1966 / Basic Books, New York, 1966)

* * * *

H. Braverman

Labor and Monopoly Capital: the degradation of work in the twentieth century (Monthly Review Press, London, New York, 1974)

M. Kranzberg &
W.H. Davenport (eds.)

Technology and Culture: an anthology (Schocken Books, New York, 1972)

D.S. Landes

The Unbound Prometheus: technological change and industrial development in western Europe from 1750 to the present (Cambridge University Press, Cambridge, 1969)

R.W. Reid

Tongues of Conscience: war and the scientists' dilemma (Constable, London, 1969 / Walker, New York, 1969)

C. Susskind

Understanding Technology (Johns Hopkins Press, Baltimore, 1973)

* * * *

R.J. Forbes

The Conquest of Nature: technology and its consequences (Pall Mall, London, 1968 / Praeger, New York, 1968)

G.M. Foster

Traditional Societies and Technological Change (Harper & Row, New York, 2nd edn, 1973)

M. Kranzberg &
C. Pursell (eds.)

Technology in Western Civilization, vol. 2, *Technology in the Twentieth Century* (Oxford University Press, London, New York, 1967)

N. Wiener   *The Human Use of Human Beings: cybernetics and society* (Eyre & Spottiswoode, London, 1950)

11 THE IMPACT OF WAR

The two world wars of the twentieth century, the mobilisation of all citizens for total war, and rapid developments in technology, have had far-reaching effects on society as a whole. The state and its political and economic institutions have also been modified by war and by the kind of armed peace that has become| accepted since 1945. Thus, where the horror of the First World War induced a widespread inclination towards pacifism in international relations, the impact of the Second was to make it possible for the organisation for war to be carried over into peacetime. This has resulted in the overriding importance for advanced economies of war production and in| the marked influence of military thinking in government policy even in 'liberal' western states. Many aspects of modern civilian life have become subject to underlying military necessities, whether these take the form of national budgeting or of the beneficial 'spin-off' (for example in medical technology) of defence spending, latterly especially in space research. Debates about the destructive use of atomic energy have been a continuous theme as technology has become more sophisticated. Even states which are not directly involved in nuclear production have been greatly influenced by its effects. Many smaller states have become clients of the larger ones in seeking to arm themselves; and in this area much great-power rivalry has turned on supplying arms to clients in strategic areas. Though no 'great' wars have been fought since armed deterrence began to govern relations between the great powers, many limited wars have taken place in which the more or less obvious presence of the clients' protectors could be discerned.

Calvocoressi, Ropp, Terraine and Wright deal with the world wars in practice, Fuller taking a long historical view of how warfare has changed, and Preston & Wise looking especially at the links between war and western society. Discussions on social effects may be found in Buchan, Foot and Howard (*Soldiers and Governments*), while Howard (*Theory and Practice* and *Studies*), Andreski, Huntington and Waltz analyse the sociological aspects of military organisation and its influence on society. The military in new states forms the theme of Janowitz and of an essay by V.G. Kiernan ('Colonial African Armies') in Bond & Roy. Reid examines the moral and social consequences of technological advance, while Blackett wrote the classic condemnation of the military use of atomic power. Brodie (*The Absolute Weapon*) reviews this question from

the perspective of the 1970s. Quester looks at nuclear diplomacy
and Martin surveys the characteristics of modern defence systems.

B. Brodie   *War and Politics* (Macmillan, London,
                                 New York, 1973)

A. Buchan   *War in Modern Society* (Harper & Row,
                                 New York, 1968)

S.E. Finer   *The Man on Horseback: the role of the
                                 military in politics* (Penguin Books,
                                 Harmondsworth, 2nd edn, 1976)

                          * * * *

B. Bond & I. Roy (eds.)   *War and Society Yearbook*, vol. 2 (Croom
                                 Helm, London, 1976 / Holmes & Meier,
                                 New York, 1977)

B. Brodie (ed.)   *The Absolute Weapon: atomic power and
                                 world order* (Books for Libraries Press,
                                 Freeport, N.Y., 1972)

M.R.D. Foot (ed.)   *War and Society* (Elek, London, 1973 /
                                 Barnes & Noble, New York, 1973)

J.F.C. Fuller   *The Conduct of War 1789-1961: a study
                                 of the impact of the French, industrial
                                 and Russian revolutions on war and its
                                 conduct* (Eyre & Spottiswoode, London,
                                 1961)

M.E. Howard   *The Theory and Practice of War: essays
                                 presented to B.H. Liddell Hart* (Cassell,
                                 London, 1965 / Praeger, New York, 1966)

S.P. Huntington   *The Changing Pattern of Military Politics*
                                 (Free Press of Glencoe, New York, 1962)

S.P. Huntington   *The Soldier and the State: the theory and
                                 politics of civil-military relations;* an essay
                                 in comparative analysis (Random House,

New York, 1964)

M. Janowitz   *The Military in the Political Development of New Nations* (University of Chicago Press, Chicago, 1964)

R.A. Preston &   *Men in Arms: a history of warfare and its*
S.F. Wise (eds.)   *interrelationships with western society* (Praeger, New York, 2nd edn, 1970)

R.W. Reid   *Tongues of Conscience: war and the scientists' dilemma* (Constable, London, 1969 / Walker, New York, 1969)

T. Ropp   *War in the Modern World* (Duke University Press, Durham, N.C., 1959 / Cambridge University Press, Cambridge, 1960)

* * * *

S. Andreski   *Military Organization and Society* (Routledge & Kegan Paul, London, 2nd edn, 1968 / University of California Press, Berkeley, 1968)

P.M.S. Blackett   *Military and Political Consequences of Atomic Energy* (Turnstile Press, London, 1948 / Folcroft Library Editions, Folcroft, Penn., 1948)

P.M.S. Blackett   *Atomic Weapons and East-West Relations* (Cambridge University Press, Cambridge, 1956)

P. Calvocoressi & G. Wint   *Total War: [the story of World War II] causes and courses of the second world war* (Allen Lane, London, 1972 / Pantheon Books, New York, 1972)

S.P. Cohen   *The Indian Army: its contribution to the development of a nation* (University of California Press, Berkeley, 1971)

M.E. Howard

Studies in War and Peace (Temple Smith, London, 1970 / Viking Press, New York, 1971)

M.E. Howard (ed.)

Soldiers and Governments: nine studies in civil-military relations (Eyre & Spottiswoode, London, 1957 / Indiana University Press, Bloomington, 1959)

M. Janowitz

Military Institutions and Coercion in the Developing Nations (University of Chicago Press, Chicago, 1977)

L.W. Martin

Arms and Strategy: an international survey of modern defence (Weidenfeld & Nicolson, London, 1973)

G.H. Quester

Nuclear Diplomacy: the first twenty-five years (Dunellen, New York, 1970)

J. Terraine

Impacts of War, 1914 and 1918 (Hutchinson, London, 1970)

K.N. Waltz

Man, the State and War: a theoretical analysis (Columbia University Press, New York, 1959 / Oxford University Press, London, 1960)

G. Wright

The Ordeal of Total War 1939-1945 (Harper & Row, New York, 1968)

12 THE PROBLEM OF POLITICAL DEVELOPMENT

The study of political development grew in the USA during the 1960s
as an aspect of the study of modernisation. It flourished on the use of
the comparative method and the need to explain why the politics of
many developing countries were so unstable. Among the questions
asked in the subject were: why do revolutions occur? why do the
military intervene so frequently in politics? what is the role of political
parties and democratic competitive politics in producing political
stability? is corruption really a bad thing? can traditional values and
institutions perform 'modern' functions? And so on . . . For some
experts the process of political development has come to acquire distinct
characteristics. It means: an increased centralisation of power in the
state coupled with the weakening of traditional sources of authority; the
differentiation and specialisation of political institutions; and increased
popular participation in politics combined with greater identification
of individuals with the political system as a whole. One point to note
here is that this definition of political development falls into the
'modernity' and 'tradition' trap; it suggests that there is essentially one
model of 'modernity' which is primarily a western one. A second point
is that there is some doubt as to the real value of the concept of political
development. Military regimes thrive in many countries in Asia, Africa
and Latin America and *ipso facto* political development has come to a
halt. Indeed, it may be more pertinent to consider the problem of political order rather than that of political development. Aspects of the
subject can be pursued further in the sections on *Religion and the
Modern State* (8), *Modernisation and 'Tradition'* (9), *Revolution* (13),
and *Terrorism* (14).

Welch's reader, though typical of the western-orientated concerns of
US political science in the 1960s, introduces important problems;
Huntington's masterpiece explains political instability in terms of the
lag in the development of effective political institutions behind social
and economic change. The works by Almond & Coleman, Pye &
Verba, Binder and Apter are all significant products of the US political
science school of the 1960s. Smith's two books and Rustow (*World of
Nations*) have much to tell of the legitimising role of tradition in political development. Andreski, Finer and Huntington (*Soldier and State*)
are important works on the relationship between military organisation

57

and society. Johnson is a useful collection of essays on the military in politics; Gutteridge, Haddad and Welch offer further studies of specific areas. Heeger feels that the study of political order would be more appropriate than the study of political development; he would approve too of the extent to which Bill & Leiden and especially Tambiah are aware of the power of traditional political institutions and forms of behaviour in the present. The remaining works are a small selection from the vast range on specific societies.

S.P. Huntington

Political Order in Changing Societies (Yale University Press, New Haven, 1968)

C.E. Welch (ed.)

Political Modernization: a reader in comparative political change (Wadsworth, Belmont, Cal., 2nd edn, 1970)

* * * *

G.A. Almond & J.S. Coleman (eds.)

The Politics of the Developing Areas (Oxford University Press, London, 1960 / Princeton University Press, Princeton, 1960)

S. Andreski

Military Organization and Society (Routledge & Kegan Paul, London, 2nd edn, 1968 / University of California Press, Berkeley, 2nd edn, 1968)

D.E. Apter

The Politics of Modernization (University of Chicago Press, Chicago, 1965)

L. Binder *et al.*

Crises and Sequences in Political Development (Princeton University Press, Princeton, 1971)

C.E. Black

The Dynamics of Modernization: a study in comparative history (Harper & Row, New York, 1967)

S.E. Finer

The Man on Horseback: the role of the military in politics (Penguin Books,

Harmondsworth, 2nd edn, 1976)

C. Geertz (ed.)
Old Societies and New States: the quest for modernity in Asia and Africa (Free Press of Glencoe, New York, 1963 / Collier-Macmillan, London, 1964)

G.A. Heeger
The Politics of Underdevelopment (Macmillan, London, 1974 / St. Martin's Press, New York, 1974)

S.P. Huntington
The Soldier and State: the theory and politics of civil-military relations; an essay in comparative analysis (Random House, New York, 1964)

M. Janowitz
The Military in the Political Development of New Nations (University of Chicago Press, Chicago, 1964)

J.J. Johnson (ed.)
The Role of the Military in Underdeveloped Countries (Princeton University Press, Princeton, 1962)

H.G. Kebschull (ed.)
Politics in Transitional Societies: the challenge of change in Asia, Africa and Latin America (Appleton-Century-Crofts, New York, 2nd edn, 1973 / Prentice-Hall International, Hemel Hempstead, 1974)

C. Leys (ed.)
Politics and Change in Developing Countries: studies in the theory and practice of development (Cambridge University Press, Cambridge, 1969)

L. Pye & S. Verba
Political Culture and Political Development (Princeton University Press, Princeton, 1965)

D.A. Rustow
A World of Nations: problems of political modernization (Brookings Inst., Washington, 1967)

D.E. Smith   *Religion and Political Development*
                                    (Little, Brown, Boston, 1970)

D.E. Smith (ed.)   *Religion, Politics and Social Change in
                                    the Third World: a sourcebook* (Free
                                    Press, New York, 1971)

                                    * * * *

J.A. Bill & C. Leiden   *The Middle East: politics and power*
                                    (Allyn & Bacon, Boston, 1974)

L. Binder   *Iran: political development in a changing
                                    society* (Cambridge University Press,
                                    Cambridge, 1962 / University of Cali-
                                    fornia Press, Berkeley, 1962)

J. Gittings   *The Role of the Chinese Army* (Oxford
                                    University Press, London, New York,
                                    1967)

W.F. Gutteridge   *The Military in African Politics* (Methuen,
                                    London, 1969 / Barnes & Noble, New
                                    York, 1969)

W.F. Gutteridge   *Military Regimes in Africa* (Methuen,
                                    London, 1975 / Harper & Row, New
                                    York, 1975)

G.M. Haddad   *Revolutions and Military Rule in the
                                    Middle East: I The Northern Tier, II The
                                    Arab States, III The Arab States Part 2;
                                    Egypt, The Sudan, Yemen and Libya*
                                    (Robert Speller, New York, 1965-1973)

J.J. Johnson   *The Military and Society in Latin America*
                                    (Stanford University Press, Stanford,
                                    1965)

R.A. Potash   *The Army and Politics in Argentina*
                                    (Stanford University Press, Stanford,
                                    1969)

L.I. & S.H. Rudolph	*The Modernity of Tradition: political development in India* (University of Chicago Press, Chicago, 1967)
A.C. Stepan	*The Military in Politics: changing patterns in Brazil* (Princeton University Press, Princeton, 1971)
S.J. Tambiah	*World Conqueror and World Renouncer: a study of Buddhism and polity in Thailand against a historical background* (Cambridge University Press, Cambridge, 1976)
K. Von Vorys	*Political Development in Pakistan* (Princeton University Press, Princeton, 1965)
R.E. Ward (ed.)	*Political Development in Modern Japan* (Princeton University Press, Princeton, 1968)
R.E. Ward & D.A. Rustow (eds.)	*Political Modernization in Japan and Turkey* (Princeton University Press, Princeton, 1964)
C.E. Welch (ed.)	*Soldier and State in Africa: a comparative analysis of military intervention and political change* (Northwestern University Press, Evanston, 1970)

13 REVOLUTION

This is a particularly contentious subject; the historical explanation of revolutions is often confused by ideological commitment. Questions to consider are: what is a revolution and what is the nature of twentieth-century revolutions? to what extent have twentieth-century revolutions been preceded or followed by major social changes? what role has been played in them by ideology, nationalist and marxist? and how have peasants come to be involved in them?

Johnson offers a typology of revolutions and Calvert examines the historical development of the concept of revolution. Particularly useful as an introduction, however, is Dunn's analysis of eight modern revolutions from the point of view of the historian and the political theorist: his book also has a valuable bibliography. Moore offers the insights of a social historian, Huntington those of a political scientist, Wolf those of an anthropologist, while Wolfenstein takes leading revolutionaries to the psychiatrist's couch. Chaliand in a *tour d'horizon* of revolutions in the non-industrial world emphasises the limited achievement of many revolutions. Migdal and Lewis offer explanations of how peasants have become involved in revolutionary movements. There is, finally, a list of titles on specific twentieth-century revolutions. Bianco is a particularly good introduction to the Chinese revolution and Hinton demonstrates what the revolution meant in one village. Race tells why Vietnamese peasants joined the Vietcong and Kahin's book is a classic study of a nationalist revolution.

P. Calvert

Revolution (Pall Mall, London, 1970 / Praeger, New York, 1970)

J. Dunn

Modern Revolutions: an introduction to the analysis of a political phenomenon (Cambridge University Press, Cambridge, 1972)

C.A. Johnson

Revolution and the Social System (Hoover Inst., Stanford, 1964)

* * * *

C.E. Black — *The Dynamics of Modernization: a study in comparative history* (Harper & Row, New York, 1967)

F.J. Carrier — *The Third World Revolutions* (Grüner, Amsterdam, 1976)

G. Chaliand — *Revolution in the Third World: myths and prospects* (Harvester, Hassocks, 1977 / Viking Press, New York, 1977)

H.M. Enzensberger (tr. M. Roloff) — *Raids and Reconstructions: essays on politics, crime and culture* (Pluto Press, London, 1976)

S.P. Huntington — *Political Order in Changing Societies* (Yale University Press, New Haven, 1968)

J.W. Lewis (ed.) — *Peasant Rebellions in Communist Asia* (Stanford University Press, Stanford, 1974)

J.S. Migdal — *Peasants, Politics and Revolution: pressures towards political and social change in the third world* (Princeton University Press, Princeton, 1975)

B. Moore — *The Social Origins of Dictatorship and Democracy: lord and peasant in the making of the modern world* (Penguin Books, Harmondsworth, 1967 / Beacon Press, Boston, 1969)

E.R. Wolf — *Peasant Wars of the Twentieth Century* (Harper & Row, New York, 1969 / Faber, London, 1971)

E.V. Wolfenstein — *The Revolutionary Personality: Lenin, Trotsky, Gandhi* (Princeton University Press, Princeton, 1967)

* * * *

L. Bianco (tr. M. Bell)   *Origins of the Chinese Revolution 1915-1949* (Stanford University Press, Stanford, 1971 / Oxford University Press, London, 1972)

C.E. Black &   *Communism and Revolution: the strategic*
T.P. Thornton (eds.)   *uses of political violence* (Princeton University Press, Princeton, 1964)

P. Calvert   *A Study of Revolution* (Clarendon Press, Oxford, 1970)

H.F. Cline   *Mexico: revolution to evolution, 1940-1960* (Oxford University Press, London, New York, 1962)

C.C. Cumberland   *Mexico: the struggle for modernity* (Oxford University Press, London, New York, 1968)

W. Hinton   *Fanshen: a documentary of revolution in a Chinese village* (Vintage Books, New York, 1968 / Penguin Books, Harmondsworth, 1972)

E.J. Hobsbawm   *Revolutionaries: contemporary essays* (Weidenfeld & Nicolson, London, 1973 / Pantheon Books, New York, 1973)

C.A. Johnson   *Revolutionary Change* (University of London Press, London, 1968)

G. McT. Kahin   *Nationalism and Revolution in Indonesia* (Cornell University Press, Ithaca, 1952)

J.T. McAlister   *Vietnam: the origins of revolution* (Allen Lane, London, 1969 / Knopf, New York, 1969)

J.M. Malloy	*Bolivia: the uncompleted revolution* (University of Pittsburgh Press, Pittsburgh, 1971)
H.L. Matthews	*Revolution in Cuba: an essay in understanding* (Scribner, New York, 1975)
J. Race	*War Comes to Long An: revolutionary conflict in a Vietnamese province* (University of California Press, Berkeley, 1972)
R.E. Ruiz	*Cuba: the making of a revolution* (University of Massachusetts Press, Amherst, 1968)
A. Suarez (tr. J. Carmichael & A. Halperin)	*Cuba: Castroism and Communism 1959-1966* (MIT Press, Cambridge, Mass., 1967)
J. Womack	*Zapata and the Mexican Revolution* (Knopf, New York, 1969 / Penguin Books, Harmondsworth, 1972)

14 TERRORISM

Terrorism is, perhaps, too immediate and pressing a problem to be considered a proper subject for academic concern. Consider, however, the significance of the activities of the radical patriots in Japan before the Second World War, that of the IRA throughout the century, that of Irgun in Palestine before 1948, that of the various Palestinian terrorist groups since 1948. Their capacity to bring about a shift in attitudes, to influence events, even to change the course of history is undeniable, and these are but a few of the organisations which have used terror in the twentieth century. So far, this important subject which forms part of the problem of political development, and lies close to the heart of that of revolution, has received too little scholarly attention. Nevertheless, on one point students of the subject are agreed: terrorists are not the same thing as guerrillas. The latter may deploy terror as a tactic, but they also often fight according to the conventions of war, exchanging prisoners and respecting the rights of non-combatants. But terrorists use any means to gain their ends: they engage in widespread assassination and excite general terror amongst the civilian population, and for this reason their achievements are indiscriminate in their effects, arbitrary and unpredictable, barbarous and inhumane, and without moral constraint. Moreover, one student of the subject, Wilkinson, has postulated the existence of three main types of politically motivated terrorism: the first is the repressive terrorism deployed primarily by states to suppress groups of individuals; the second the use of terror for all but a revolutionary seizure of power i.e. for intimidation or for vengeance; and the third use of terror with the long-term objective of bringing about a political revolution and perhaps changes in the socio-economic order. Questions of interest to historians, as well as to scholars in other disciplines, are: how important has been the use of terror in particular historical contexts? in what conditions do terrorists thrive? what sort of people become terrorists? do the terrorist traditions of particular societies, for instance those of Ireland, Japan, or the West Bengal state of India, help legitimise fresh terrorist groups when they emerge? what part is played by ideology in generating terrorist activity? and why has terrorism acquired an international dimension in recent years?

A good introduction to this subject has yet to be written. Nevertheless Laqueur and Wilkinson (*Terrorism and the Liberal State*) are useful, the former's book being written from an historian's angle and the latter's from that of a political scientist. Hyams has written a lightweight but readable account of many aspects of terrorism in the twentieth century, and is concerned to emphasise its effectiveness as a weapon. The works edited by Alexander and Carlton & Schaerf on international terrorism are both comprehensive in their scope. Debray, Guevara, Marighela and Fanon have all written books of importance in moulding terrorist beliefs, while the biographical statements of terrorists such as Grivas, Begin and Khaled are useful for acquiring insight into the conditions which bred them. Storry's book is the classic study of the Japanese terrorists of the 1930s; Chaliand provides background to the Palestinian Arabs. Paget gives a first-hand account of what it was like, in the process of decolonisation, to be on the receiving end of a terrorist campaign. Clutterbuck and Bowden are concerned primarily with the lessons to be learned from different terrorist campaigns by state security systems.

W.Z. Laqueur	*Terrorism* (Weidenfeld & Nicolson, London, 1977 / Little, Brown, Waltham, Mass., 1977)
P. Wilkinson	*Terrorism and the Liberal State* (Macmillan, London, 1977)
	* * * *
Y. Alexander (ed.)	*International Terrorism: national, regional and global perspectives* (Praeger, New York, 1976)
D. Carlton & C. Schaerf (eds.)	*International Terrorism and World Security* (Croom Helm, London, 1975 / Halsted Press, New York, 1975)
E. Hyams	*Terrorists and Terrorism* (Dent, London, 1975 / St. Martin's Press, New York, 1975)
P. Wilkinson	*Political Terrorism* (Macmillan, London, 1974)

* * * *

M. Begin (tr. S. Katz) | *The Revolt [: story of the Irgun]* (W.H. Allen, London, 1951 / Schuman, New York, 1951)

T. Bowden | *The Breakdown of Public Security: the case of Ireland 1916-1921 and Palestine 1936-1939* (Sage, London, Beverly Hills, 1977)

G. Chaliand | *The Palestinian Resistance* (Penguin Books, Harmondsworth, 1972)

R. Clutterbuck | *Protest and the Urban Guerilla* (Cassell, London, 1973)

R. Clutterbuck | *Guerillas and Terrorists* (Faber, London, 1977)

R. Debray (tr. B. Ortis) | *Revolution in the Revolution?* (Penguin Books, Harmondsworth, 1967 / Monthly Review Press, New York, 1967)

F. Fanon (tr. C. Farrington) | *The Wretched of the Earth* (Grove Press, New York, 1965 / Penguin Books, Harmondsworth, 1967)

C. Foley (ed.) | *The Memoirs of General Grivas* (Cresset, London, 1964 / Praeger, New York, 1965)

C. Guevara (tr. I.F. Stone) | *Guerilla Warfare* (Vintage Books, New York, 1967 / Penguin Books, Harmondsworth, 1969)

E. Halperin | *Terrorism in Latin America* (Sage, London, Beverly Hills, 1976)

L. Khaled | *My People Shall Live: the autobiography of a Revolutionary* (Hodder & Stoughton, London, 1973)

C. Marighela   *Minimanual of the Urban Guerilla* (Penguin
                      Books, Harmondsworth, 1971)

J. Paget   *Last Post: Aden 1964-1967* (Faber,
                      London, 1969)

L. Paine   *The Terrorists* (Robert Hale, London,
                      1975)

R. Storry   *The Double Patriots* (Chatto & Windus,
                      London, 1957 / Houghton Mifflin,
                      Boston, 1957)

15 POPULATION

Most books on population begin with Malthus and his anxieties about its growth in the early nineteenth century, and this helps to balance contemporary preoccupations: it is not growth as such but the scale and rapidity of the increase that makes population an important twentieth-century theme. The causes of the expansion are one facet of the study of population; the effects are of greater moment since they have affected society and government in the widest sense very profoundly. Ecological concerns assumed prominence with the post-1950 realisation that the earth's resources are finite. Power and wealth have ensured that a greater share has been secured by richer states, and the fact that the poorer areas have grown steadily poorer, relatively, has forced itself upon the attention of the world community because population pressure is greatest in some of the poorest regions. But apart from this global consideration, political and social effects at more local levels have been far-reaching. With huge populations to manage, techniques of control have tended to become more uniform and more authoritarian and government agencies have become more remote. This has diminished the role of the individual in the extent to which he can influence his own environment. Perhaps the most important questions to ask, after that of how to survive, are: how well has democracy adapted itself to functioning on a scale for which it was never intended? what has been the effect of massive numbers on the creation and maintenance of a national identity in states both new and old? to what extent has migration from crowded into 'empty' spaces offered a solution and what have been the effects of migrations on social, political and economic structures in the host countries as well as on the migrants' polities?

Organski makes an excellent introduction to the theme of world population problems, taking a world-wide perspective and placing the twentieth century in its historical context. Heer's short work seeks to answer the question of why population matters to society and therefore to the historian. Borrie also looks at this question and has chapters on the special problems of the Third World and on the wide political and social implications of population growth. These matters, and the global nature of population problems in the twentieth century, are taken up by Symonds & Carder. This study is especially interesting because it

70

examines the way in which the United Nations has approached the task
of attempting to offer solutions. Thompson & Lewis takes a long view
of population growth in space and time and has some useful definitions
of population pressure. The sociological approach of Matras is full of
insights about participation in government, internal and international
migration and national identity. The relationship between population
and welfare is dealt with by Spengler; and Clark, though more technical,
places the twentieth century on a time scale. A similar perspective
may be gained from reading Carr-Saunders, written in the 1930s before
the dimension of the contemporary population explosion was generally
appreciated.

D.M. Heer   *Society and Population* (Prentice-Hall,
                                 Englewood Cliffs, 1968)

C. McEvedy & R. Jones   *Atlas of World Population History*
(eds.)   (Allen Lane, London, 1978)

T. McKeown   * *The Modern Rise of Population* (Edward
                                 Arnold, London, 1976)

K. & A.F.K. Organski   *Population and World Power* (Knopf,
                                 New York, 1961)

                                 * * * *

W.D. Borrie   *The Growth and Control of World Popu-
                                 lation* (Weidenfeld & Nicolson, London,
                                 1970)

J.I. Clarke   *Population Geography and the Developing
                                 Countries* (Pergamon, Oxford, New York,
                                 1971)

P.R. & A.H. Ehrlich   *Population Resources Environment:
                                 issues in human ecology* (W.H. Freeman,
                                 Reading, San Francisco, 2nd edn, 1972)

B. Harvey & J.D. Hallett   *Environment and Society: an introductory
                                 analysis* (Macmillan, London, 1977 / MIT
                                 Press, Cambridge, Mass., 1977)

H.B. Parry (ed.) — *Population and its Problems: a plain man's guide* (Clarendon Press, Oxford, 1970)

R. Symonds & M. Carder — *The United Nations and the Population Question 1945-1970* (Chatto & Windus, London, 1973)

W.S. Thompson & D.T. Lewis — *Population Problems* (McGraw-Hill, New York, 5th edn, 1965)

E.A. Wrigley — *Population and History* (Weidenfeld & Nicolson, London, 1969 / McGraw-Hill, New York, 1969)

* * * *

A.M. Carr-Saunders — *World Population: past growth and present trends* (Clarendon Press, Oxford, 1936)

S. Chandrasekhar (ed.) — *Asia's Population Problems: with a discussion of population and immigration in Australia* (Allen & Unwin, London, 1967 / Praeger, New York, 1967)

D. Chaplin (ed.) — *Population Policies and Growth in Latin America* (Lexington Books, Lexington, Mass., 1971)

C. Clark — *Population Growth and Land Use* (Macmillan, London, 1967 / St. Martin's Press, New York, 1967)

W.A. Hance — *Population, Migration, and Urbanization in Africa* (Columbia University Press, New York, 1970)

S.F. Hartley — *Population Quantity vs. Quality: a sociological examination of the causes and consequences of the population explosion* (Prentice-Hall, Englewood Cliffs, 1972)

P.M. Hauser (ed.) — *The Population Dilemma* (Prentice-Hall,

	Englewood Cliffs, 2nd edn, 1969)
J. Matras	*Introduction to Population: a sociological approach* (Prentice-Hall, Englewood Cliffs, 1977)
J. Spengler	*Population Change, Modernization and Welfare* (Prentice-Hall, Englewood Cliffs, 1974)
L. Tabah (ed.)	*Population Growth and Economic Development in the Third World* 2 vols. (Ordina Eds., Dolhain, Belgium, 1975)
E. Thomlinson	*Population Dynamics: causes and consequences of world demographic change* (Random House, New York, 1965)

URBANISATION

It is important to view urbanisation in its historical perspective: cities have existed for millenia and have nurtured the growth of states and civilisations. The features which distinguish the cities of the twentieth century are: first, the scale and rapidity of their growth; second, that this growth has taken place in economies which can ill afford large numbers of unproductive citizens; and third, that the imbalance resulting from both these factors has tended to create an environment which is socially alienating rather than integrative and in which expectations of economic betterment or of an intangible 'quality of life' have not been fulfilled. Nevertheless, cities have continued to act as powerful solvents of class and culture and have cradled nationalist movements in many new states where the influence of urban elites has led to extremes of tension between town and country. By contrast, in some of the more highly industrialised areas, where class and racial barriers have become more sharply pronounced, cities have tended to be divisive, the ultimate exemplar being urban *apartheid* in South Africa, but coloured and cultural 'ghettos' have also developed in western cities. Poverty and unemployment among city dwellers in Third World countries have given rise to urban masses that are potentially revolutionary and for this reason alone authoritarian governments have emerged, seeking to extend their control in the interests of 'order'. But such matters as health, communications, education, leisure and administrative machinery, which in cities cannot easily be ignored, have also led to considerable increase of state intervention in the activities of individuals.

Lowry provides a straightforward introduction to the subject for the non-specialist. Davis, in both works, takes a long view of the city in history, while Mumford, going back to earlier centuries and devoting only the last section to the twentieth century in *The City in History,* makes some biting criticisms of modern trends in urbanisation. Hauser & Schnore has a very good introduction, draws useful and enlightening comparisons between western and Third World cities in Part II, and concludes soundly on an historical note. Handlin & Burchard, though mainly about cities in the west, asks questions which are generally applicable to the role of the city in society. McGee is specially useful in that it takes the model of western cities and places this against the

realities of cities in the Third World. Mangin's *Readings* illustrate anthro-
pological problems of urbanisation which are also dealt with by Southall.
The two books by Dwyer are important studies of cities in the Third
World, while Hall is an authority on the subject of urbanisation.

F.J. Coppa & P.C. Dolce	*Cities in Transition: from the ancient world to urban America* (Nelson-Hall, Chicago, 1974)
K. Davis (ed.)	*Cities: Their Origin, Growth and Human Impact; readings from 'Scientific American'* (W.H. Freeman, San Francisco, 1973)
P. Hall	*The World Cities* (McGraw-Hill, New York, 1966 / Weidenfeld & Nicolson, London, 2nd edn, 1977)
R. Jones (ed.)	*Essays on World Urbanization* (G. Philip & Son, London, 1975)
J.H. Lowry	*World City Growth* (Edward Arnold, London, 1975)

* * * *

R.P. Beckinsale & J.M. Houston (eds.)	*Urbanization and its Problems: essays in honour of E.W. Gilbert* (Blackwell, Oxford, 1968 / Barnes & Noble, New York, 1968)
D.J. Dwyer	*The City in the Third World* (Barnes & Noble, New York, 1968 / Macmillan, London, 1974)
T.G. McGee	*The Urbanization Process in the Third World: explorations in search of a theory* (Bell, London, 1971)

W. Mangin (ed.)	*Peasants in Cities: readings in the anthropology of urbanization* (Houghton Mifflin, Boston, 1970)
L. Mumford	*The City in History: its origins, its transformations, and its prospects* (Secker & Warburg, London, 1961 / Harcourt Brace, New York, 1961)
L. Mumford	*The Urban Prospect* (Secker & Warburg, London, 1968 / Harcourt Brace & World, 1968)
R.E. Pahl	*Patterns of Urban Life* (Longman, Harlow, 1970 / Humanities Press, New York, 1970)
A. Southall (ed.)	*Urban Anthropology: cross-cultural studies of urbanization* (Oxford University Press, New York, 1973)
W.D.C. Wright & P.H. Steward	*The Exploding City* (Edinburgh University Press, Edinburgh, 1972)

* * * *

B.J.L. Berry	*The Human Consequences of Urbanization: divergent paths in the urban experience of the twentieth century* (Macmillan, London, 1973 / St. Martin's Press, New York, 1973)
G.W. Breese	*Urbanization in Newly-Developing Countries* (Prentice-Hall, Englewood Cliffs, 1966)
T. Chandler & G. Fox	*3000 Years of Urban Growth* (Academic Press, London, New York, 1974)
K. Davis	*World Urbanization 1950-1970* 2 vols. (California Inst. of International Studies, University of California, Berkeley, 1969-72)

R.E. Dickinson   *The West European City: a geographical interpretation* (Routledge & Kegan Paul, London, 1951)

D.J. Dwyer (ed.)   *The City as a Centre of Change in Asia* (Hong Kong University Press, Hong Kong, 1972)

T.H. Elkins   *The Urban Explosion* (Macmillan, London, 1973 / Humanities Press, New York, 1973)

J. Gottman (ed.)   *Megalopolis: the urbanized northeastern seaboard of the United States* (Twentieth Century Fund, New York, 1962)

P. Hall (ed.)   *Europe 2000* (Duckworth, London, 1977)

W.A. Hance   *Population, Migration, and Urbanization in Africa* (Columbia University Press, New York, 1970)

C. Handlin & J. Burchard (eds.)   *The Historian and the City* (MIT Press, Cambridge, Mass., 1963)

P.M. Hauser & L.F. Schnore (eds.)   *The Study of Urbanization* (John Wiley, New York, 1965)

G.K. Payne   *Urban Housing in the Third World* (Leonard Hill, London, 1977 / Routledge & Kegan Paul, Boston, 1977)

17 ENERGY: THE POLITICAL DIMENSION

The industrialised world depends for its survival upon continuous and increasing supplies of energy and even the least developed areas cannot do without them. King Coal was largely supplanted by the second half of the twentieth century by petroleum; atomic energy, though it has featured in public debate for its military and ecological dangers, has not begun to produce a substantial part of the world's energy requirements. Political and economic domination of oil-bearing regions has accompanied the exploitation of petroleum by developed economies since the early years of the present century. But only in the post-1945 era has oil assumed major importance in the politics as well as in the economies of the world, a role dramatically underlined by the capacity of OPEC, the oil-producers' cartel, to dictate prices which had grave consequences for capitalist economies everywhere. The appreciation that the resources of the earth are finite also stimulated public debate and prompted attempts to influence government policy on the uses of energy.

Odell (*Oil and World Power*) ranges over the whole field of the exploitation and marketing of oil and natural gas and makes an excellent introduction to the subject, as does Tugendhat & Hamilton which begins with an interesting historical account. The intimate connection between governments and oil companies is brought out in Hartshorn while Turner discusses the world-wide ramifications of the oil industry, a theme treated in a meticulously scholarly way by Penrose. OPEC is discussed in several works, notably Al-Otaiba, Stone and Stork. Stone also looks at the changes wrought by sudden wealth on the societies of the Middle East. Hurewitz should be read for an account of the effect of oil politics on the Arab-Israel dispute; and oil and foreign policy is the subject of Mosley, Shwadran, and, especially, Klebanoff. The much-debated issues involved in nuclear power are the subject of Patterson, written for the non-specialist; so is Foley which considers all forms of energy in the modern world.

G. Foley with C. Nassim *The Energy Question* (Penguin Books, Harmondsworth, 1976)

P.R. Odell · *Oil and World Power: background to the oil crisis* (Penguin Books, Harmondsworth, 4th edn, 1974)

C. Tugendhat & A. Hamilton · *Oil the Biggest Business* (Eyre Methuen, London, rev. edn, 1975)

* * * *

P.S.M. Blackett · *The Military and Political Consequences of Atomic Energy* (Turnstile Press, London, 1948 / Folcroft Library Editions, Folcroft, Penn., 1948)

J.E. Hartshorn · *Oil Companies and Governments: an account of the international oil industry in its political environment* (Faber, London, 2nd edn, 1967)

J.E. Hartshorn · *Politics and World Oil Economics: an account of the international oil industry in its political environment* (Praeger, New York, rev. edn, 1967)

J.C. Hurewitz (ed.) · *Oil, the Arab-Israel Dispute and the Industrial World: horizons of crisis* (Westview Press, Boulder, Col., 1976)

N.H. Jacoby · *Multinational Oil: a study in industrial dynamics* (Macmillan, New York, 1974 / Collier-Macmillan, London, 1975)

S. Klebanoff · *Middle East Oil and U.S. Foreign Policy: with special reference to the energy crisis* (Pall Mall, London, 1974 / Praeger, New York, 1974)

L. Mosley · *Power Play: the tumultuous world of Middle East oil 1890-1973* (Weidenfeld & Nicolson, London, 1973)

P.R. Odell   *An Economic Geography of Oil* (Bell,
                      London, 1963 / Greenwood Press, West-
                      port, Conn., 1974)

B. Shwadran   *The Middle East, Oil and the Great
                      Powers* (John Wiley, New York, 3rd edn,
                      1973)

J. Stork   *Middle East Oil and the Energy Crisis*
                      (Monthly Review Press, New York, 1975)

                      * * * *

M. Abir   *Oil, Power and Politics: conflict in Arabia,
                      the Red Sea and the Gulf* (Frank Cass,
                      London, 1974)

M.S. Al-Otaiba   *OPEC and the Petroleum Industry* (Croom
                      Helm, London, 1975)

C. Issawi &   *The Economics of Middle Eastern Oil*
M. Yeganeh   (Faber, London, 1962 / Praeger, New
                      York, 1963)

Z. Mikdashi   *The Community of Oil Exporting Countries:
                      a study in governmental co-operation*
                      (Allen & Unwin, London, 1972 / Cornell
                      University Press, Ithaca, 1972)

W.C. Patterson   *Nuclear Power* (Penguin Books, Harmonds-
                      worth, 1976)

E. Penrose   *The Large International Firm in Develop-
                      ing Countries: the international petroleum
                      industry* (Allen & Unwin, London, 1968 /
                      MIT Press, Cambridge, Mass., 1969)

W.R. Polk   *The United States and the Arab World*
                      (Oxford University Press, London, 1975 /
                      Harvard University Press, Cambridge,
                      Mass., 3rd edn, 1975)

R.A. Stone (ed.)   *OPEC and the Middle East: the impact of oil on societal development* (Praeger, New York, 1977)

L. Turner   *Invisible Empires: multinational companies and the modern world* (Hamilton, London, 1970 / Harcourt Brace Jovanovich, New York, 1971)

18 RACE AND COLOUR

There are several aspects of this theme. First, the twentieth century has inherited the legacy of the age of empire, in which was assumed the 'superiority' of the dominant races and the 'inferiority' of the subordinate ones. Second, people from poor countries of the Third World, seeking new opportunities and an escape from poverty, have migrated to richer 'white' areas in numbers sufficiently large for awareness of racial differences (perhaps essentially cultural or economic) to be enhanced, and to create problems of assimilation for these 'alien' groups. Third, coloured peoples themselves have demanded greater recognition in the world and equality within national states. This took shape as *negritude* in Africa, and as the 'black is beautiful' and the Civil Rights movements in the USA and in demands for independence in Asia and Africa. A fourth variant is the institutionalisation of the colour bar (for political and economic reasons) in South Africa; this case seems to continue the pattern of imperialism through the domination of a white minority. In general, the attempt to discover the historical and sociological bases of racial prejudice, and to investigate the peaceful and violent attempts that have been made to overcome it or enforce it, is the subject of this section. Of course, racial prejudice has not been confined to groups of different colour; the example of Nazi Germany and the many different grounds on which persecution has taken place throughout the world bears witness to this.

Banton's books give a firm grounding in the subject with both theoretical approaches and practical examples from all over the world. Irvine bases his discussion on the effects of European domination of non-European territories, treating the subject historically and devoting the last section to the twentieth century. Kiernan writes about the imperial experience with authority. Kuper, using analytical techniques, and Mason, more descriptive, are both useful. Benedict, a noted anthropologist, discusses racial prejudice from the viewpoint of that discipline. Wilson draws an interesting contrast between American Negroes and South African Blacks. Fanon's polemic about Algerians under French rule is filled with emotional overtones. The extent to which race has become an international issue is considered by Tinker.

M. Banton   *Race Relations* (Tavistock Publications, London, 1967 / Basic Books, New York, 1967)

K. Irvine   *The Rise of the Coloured Races* (Allen & Unwin, London, 1972)

P. Worsley   *The Third World* (Weidenfeld & Nicolson, London, 2nd edn, 1967 / University of Chicago Press, Chicago, 1970)

* * * *

R. Benedict   *Race and Racism* (Routledge, London, 1942)

R. Benedict   *Race: Science and Politics* (Viking Press, New York, 1959)

T. Draper   *The Rediscovery of Black Nationalism* (Viking Press, New York, 1970 / Secker & Warburg, London, 1971)

F. Fanon   *The Wretched of the Earth* (Grove Press,
(tr. C. Farrington)   New York, 1965 / Penguin Books, Harmondsworth, 1967)

V.G. Kiernan   *The Lords of Human Kind: European attitudes towards the outside world in the Imperial Age* (Weidenfeld & Nicolson, London, 1969)

V.G. Kiernan   *The Lords of Human Kind: black man, yellow man and white man in an age of empire* (Little, Brown, Boston, 1969)

P. Mason   *Patterns of Dominance* (Oxford University Press, London, New York, 1970)

H. Tinker   *Race, Conflict and the International Order: from empire to United Nations* (Macmillan, London, 1977)

* * * *

M. Banton   *The Idea of Race* (Tavistock Publications, London, 1977)

E.L. Bergen   *Labour, Race and Colonial Rule: the copperbelt from 1924 to independence* (Clarendon Press, Oxford, 1974)

L. Kuper   *Race, Class and Power: ideology and revolutionary change in plural societies* (Duckworth, London, 1974 / Aldine Pub. Co., Chicago, 1975)

H.J. & R.E. Simons   *Class and Colour in South Africa 1850-1950* (Penguin Books, Harmondsworth, 1969)

W.J. Wilson   *Power, Racism and Privilege: race relations in theoretical and socio-historical perspectives* (Collier-Macmillan, London, 1973 / Macmillan, New York, 1973)

19 EAST ASIA

The three excellent works which head the list of titles in this section embrace the whole area and provide a first-rate introduction to it. Thereafter for the purpose of this bibliography, the geographical whole is broken down into its two principal components, China and Japan. Each in turn is then observed in its foreign relations and from its domestic perspective.

G.C. Allen & A.G. Donnithorne	*Western Enterprise in Far Eastern Economic Development: China and Japan* (Allen & Unwin, London, 1958)
J.K. Fairbank, E.O. Reischauer & A.M. Craig	*East Asia: tradition and transformation* (Allen & Unwin, London, 1973 / Houghton Mifflin, Boston, 1973)
E.O. Reischauer & J.K. Fairbank	*East Asia, the Great Tradition* (Allen & Unwin, London, 1960 / Houghton Mifflin, Boston, 1960)

* * * *

China

The Chinese empire finally collapsed from within in 1912, after a century of external pressure, foreign encroachment and internal disturbance. But the Republic which followed found no easy solutions to the problems of this vast territory, still subject to civil wars, to humiliation from the west and from Japan, and having to face the enormous handicaps of poverty, underdevelopment and overpopulation. Sun Yat-Sen's idealistic programme of national rehabilitation failed to register any substantial successes. Yet retrospectively the seeds of regeneration may be detected in the vigorous May Fourth movement and in the founding of the Chinese Communist Party. The changing relationship between this revolutionary force and the Kuomintang, and the extent to which Chiang Kai-Shek neglected opportunities of reforming the country and allowed initiatives to pass to Mao and the CCP is part of the explanation of the eventual victory of the CCP in 1949. Among other elements to be considered are the role of the Japanese invaders both before and during the Second World War and the intimate association developed between communists and peasants in rural areas. Relations with the USSR need to be taken into account too: the CCP began as a mere appendage of the Soviet Union, but has profoundly influenced the course of the twentieth century by its rejection of the Russian revolutionary model and of Russian patronage.

One important problem in the history of China since 1949 is to explain the roles played by the party, the army and the bureaucracy; another problem has been the competition between different ideas as to the path the Chinese revolution should follow, a competition writ large in the Great Leap Forward, the Cultural Revolution and the struggle for the succession to Mao Tse-Tung. The path followed by the Chinese revolution has provided one of the greatest innovations in the Third World, yet the peculiar conditions and characteristics of Chinese society have ensured a considerable amount of continuity with the past. Scarcely less noteworthy was the reconciliation of China and the USA when, after more than twenty years of bitter hostility and suspicion, China was at last allowed to take her seat at the United Nations as one of the world's great powers. The Sino-Soviet split, which made this development possible, has also shown itself in the rivalry in different parts of the Third World between these two powers, especially in the 1960s, in Africa and in South-east Asia.

China and the World

Jansen (*Japan and China*) and Wang should be regarded as essential reading: both, from different points of view, provide a good introduction to China's place in and its relations with the outside world. Fitzgerald (*Chinese View*) also deals with this subject with great understanding and sympathy. Gittings gives an important overview of foreign policy. The special area of Sino-Soviet relations is dealt with by Floyd and especially by Clubb; it is instructive to weigh these accounts against Borisov and Koloskov which presents the official Soviet view. Relations between China and the USA are explored by Fairbank which is good on the Chinese side; May & Thomson also covers this topic, of which MacFarquhar provides a documentary profile. Mozingo is especially interesting on why the Chinese communists failed to establish themselves in Indonesia. Hutchinson and Van Ness look at China's adventures in support of foreign revolutionary movements in an attempt to combat Soviet influence in the Third World.

M.B. Jansen   *Japan and China: from war to peace*
                               1894-1972 (Rand McNally, Chicago, 1975)

Wang Gungwu   *China and the World Since 1949* (Mac-
                               millan, London, 1977)

                               * * * *

O.E. Clubb   *China and Russia: the 'Great Game'*
                               (Columbia University Press, New York,
                               1971)

D.J. Dallin   *Soviet Russia and the Far East* (Archon
                               Books, Hamden, Conn., 1971, reprint of
                               1948 edn)

C.P. Fitzgerald   *The Chinese View of their Place in the*
                               World (Oxford University Press, London,
                               New York, 1969)

D. Floyd   *Mao against Krushchev: a short history of*
                               the Sino-Soviet conflict (Praeger, New
                               York, 1963 / Pall Mall, London, 1964)

J. Gittings   *The World and China 1922-1972* (Methuen,
                               London, 1974 / Harper & Row, New York,
                               1974)

R.C. North   *The Foreign Relations of China* (Dickinson
                               Pub. Co., Encino, Cal., 1974)

A. Ulam   *Expansion and Co-Existence: Soviet*
                               foreign policy 1917-1973 (Praeger, New
                               York, 2nd edn, 1974)

H.M. Vinacke   *History of the Far East in Modern Times*
                               (Appleton-Century-Crofts, New York,
                               6th edn, 1959 / Allen & Unwin, London,
                               1960)

                               * * * *

O.B. Borisov &   *Soviet Chinese Relations 1945-1970*
B.T. Koloskov   (Indiana University Press, Bloomington,
(ed. V. Petrov)   1975)

J.K. Fairbank   *The United States and China* (Harvard
                      University Press, Cambridge, Mass.,
                      3rd edn, 1971)

C.P. Fitzgerald   *The Southern Expansion of the Chinese
                      People; ['southern fields and southern
                      oceans']* (Barrie & Jenkins, London,
                      1972 / Praeger, New York, 1972)

A. Hutchinson   *China's African Revolution* (Hutchinson,
                      London, 1975)

R. MacFarquhar (ed.) *Sino-American Relations 1949-1972*
                      (Praeger, New York, 1972)

E.R. May &   *American-East Asian Relations: a survey*
J.C. Thomson Jr (eds.) (Harvard University Press, Cambridge,
                      Mass., 1972)

D. Mozingo   *Chinese Policy towards Indonesia 1949-
                      1970* (Cornell University Press, Ithaca,
                      1976)

R.C. North   *Moscow and Chinese Communists* (Stan-
                      ford University Press, Stanford, 1953)

P. Van Ness   *Revolution and Chinese Foreign Policy:
                      Peking's support for wars of national
                      liberation* (University of California Press,
                      Berkeley, 1970)

China – the Domestic Perspective

Fitzgerald (*Birth of Communist China*) is a balanced explanation of the Communists' rise to power, and Bianco is also an excellent introduction.

For greater detail about the period up to 1949, Sheridan is first rate, and for the subsequent history of the CCP Thornton should be referred to. Chesnaux (*Peasant Revolts*) provides a long historical perspective on the role of peasant rebellion which Johnson deals with in a more limited period, but his views have been challenged and should be read with caution. Mao himself on 'Peasant Movement in Hunan' is not to be missed. Wright's monograph covers the earliest years of the century, leading up to the collapse of the empire; Chow Tse-Tung analyses the important May Fourth movement, and in another monograph, Schiffrin discusses Sun Yat Sen's contribution to the revolutionary movement. The history of the CCP is covered by Harrison; and North, Schurmann & Schell and Schwartz also furnish information about various aspects of the CCP. Mao himself has yet to find a worthy biographer, but Schramm, Carter, Suyin, Uhalley and Pye all give some facets of his work and character. China's economy is treated in general by Eckstein and by Perkins, and in detail by Chen & Galenson and by Myers. Snow, for long a unique, and always a sympathetic observer of Chinese communism, may be read for his early impressions in *Red Star over China* (first published in 1937) and for his views thirty years later in *Red China Today*. Further personal records are to be found in W. Hinton (*Fanshen*) who demonstrates what revolution meant in a Chinese village and Chen (*A Year in Upper Felicity*) who observed the later Cultural Revolution in a similar context. Information about the working of the revolutionary government after 1949 may be found in simple outline by Waller, and more fully in Domes, while Gittings is an authority on the Chinese army. Lewis and Lindbeck examine particular problems in depth.

L. Bianco (tr. M. Bell)	*Origins of the Chinese Revolution, 1915-1949* (Stanford University Press, Stanford, 1971 / Oxford University Press, London, 1972)
R.M. Breth	*Mao's China: a study of socialist economic development* (Longman, London, New York, 1977)
J. Chesnaux, F. Barbier & M.C. Bergère (tr. P. Auster & L. Davis)	*China from the 1911 Revolution to Liberation* (Harvester, Hassocks, 1978 / Pantheon, New York, 1978)

J. Chesnaux *et al.*   *The People's Republic of China, 1949-1976* (Harvester, Hassocks, forthcoming)

O.E. Clubb   *20th Century China* (Columbia University Press, New York, London, 2nd edn, 1972)

J. Domes   *The Internal Politics of China 1949-1972*
(tr. R. Machetzki)   (Hurst, London, 1973 / Praeger, New York, 1973)

C.P. Fitzgerald   *The Birth of Communist China* (Penguin Books, Harmondsworth, 1964 / Praeger, New York, 1964)

* * * *

P. Carter   *Mao* (Oxford University Press, London, New York, 1976)

J. Chen   *A Year in Upper Felicity: life in a Chinese village during the cultural revolution* (Collier-Macmillan, London, 1973 / Macmillan, New York, 1973)

Chow Tse-Tung   *The May Fourth Movement: intellectual revolution in modern China* (Harvard University Press, Cambridge, Mass., 1960)

A. Eckstein   *China's Economic Revolution* (Cambridge University Press, Cambridge, 1977)

C.P. Fitzgerald   *China: a short cultural history* (Cresset, London, 1935, rev. edn, 1958 / Praeger, New York, 1958)

J.P. Harrison   *The Long March to Power: a history of the Chinese communist party 1921-1972* (Praeger, New York, 1972 / Macmillan, London, 1973)

H.C. Hinton   *An Introduction to Chinese Politics* (David & Charles, Newton Abbot, 1973 /

Praeger, New York, 1973)

W. Hinton — *Fanshen: a documentary of revolution in a Chinese village* (Vintage Books, New York, 1968 / Penguin Books, Harmondsworth, 1972)

C.A. Johnson — *Peasant Nationalism and Communist Power: the emergence of revolutionary China 1937-1945* (Stanford University Press, Stanford, 1962)

Mao Tse-Tung — *Selected Works,* vol. i, 'Report on an Investigation of the Peasant Movement in Hunan', 1927 (Lawrence & Wishart, London, 1954 / International Publishers, New York, 1954)

D. & N. Milton & F. Schurmann — *People's China* (Penguin Books, Harmondsworth, 1977)

L.W. Pye — *Mao Tse-Tung: the man in the leader* (Basic Books, New York, 1976)

F. Schurmann & O. Schell — *Communist China: revolutionary reconstruction and international confrontation 1949 to the present* (Vintage Books, New York, 1976 / Penguin Books, Harmondsworth, 1978)

B.I. Schwartz — *Chinese Communism and the Rise of Mao* (Harper & Row, New York, 1967)

J.E. Sheridan — *China in Disintegration: the republican era in Chinese history 1912-1949* (Free Press, New York, 1975 / Collier-Macmillan, London, 1976)

E. Snow — *Red Star Over China* (Grove Press, New York, rev. edn, 1968 / Gollancz, London, rev. edn, 1969)

E. Snow — *Red China Today* (Penguin Books, Harmondsworth, 1970 / Random House, New York, 1971)

R.C. Thornton — *China: the Struggle for Power 1917-1972* (Indiana University Press, Bloomington, 1973)

S. Uhalley — *Mao Tse-Tung: a critical biography* (New Viewpoints, New York, 1975)

* * * *

A.D. Barnett — *Uncertain Passage: China's passage into the post-Mao era* (Brookings Inst., Washington, 1974)

N.-R. Chen & W. Galenson — *The Chinese Economy Under Communism* (Edinburgh University Press, Edinburgh, 1969 / Aldine Pub. Co., Chicago, 1969)

J. Chesneaux (tr. C.A. Curwen) — *Peasant Revolts in China 1840-1949* (Thames & Hudson, London, 1973 / Norton, New York, 1973)

J. Gittings — *The Role of the Chinese Army* (Oxford University Press, London, New York, 1967)

J.P. Harrison — *The Communists and Chinese Peasant Rebellions: a study in the rewriting of Chinese history* (Gollancz, London, 1970 / Atheneum, New York, 1970)

M.B. Jansen — *The Japanese and Sun Yat-Sen* (Stanford University Press, Stanford, 1970)

S. Karnow — *Mao and China: from revolution to revolution* (Macmillan, London, 1972 / Viking Press, New York, 1972)

J.W. Lewis — *Party Leadership and Revolutionary Power in China* (Cambridge University Press, Cambridge, 1970)

J.M.H. Lindbeck (ed.)   *China: Management of a Revolutionary Society* (University of Washington Press, Seattle, 1971 / Allen & Unwin, London, 1972)

R.H. Myers   *The Chinese Peasant Economy: agricultural development in Hopei and Shantung 1890-1949* (Harvard University Press, Cambridge, Mass., 1970)

R.C. North   *Chinese Communism* (Weidenfeld & Nicolson, London, 1966 / McGraw-Hill, New York, 1966)

D.H. Perkins (ed.)   *China's Modern Economy in Historical Perspective* (Stanford University Press, Stanford, 1975)

H.Z. Schiffrin   *Sun Yat-Sen and the Origins of the Chinese Revolution* (University of California Press, Berkeley, London, 1970)

S.R. Schramm   *Mao Tse-Tung* (Penguin Books, Harmondsworth, 1966)

S.R. Schramm   *The Political Thought of Mao Tse-Tung* (Penguin Books, Harmondsworth, 1969 / Praeger, New York, 1969)

H. Suyin   *Wind in the Tower: Mao Tse-Tung and the Chinese Revolution 1949-1975* (Cape, London, 1976 / Little, Brown, Waltham, Mass., 1976)

D.J. Waller   *The Government and Politics of Communist China* (Hutchinson, London, 1973 / Humanities Press, Atlantic Highlands, N.J., 1976)

C.M. Wilbur   *Sun Yat-Sen: frustrated patriot* (Columbia University Press, New York, 1976)

M.C. Wright (ed.)   *China in Revolution: the first phase*
                           1900-1913 (Yale University Press, New
                           Haven, 1968)

Japan

Japan's relations with the world divide naturally at 1945. Before that
date, the emphasis lay on militant economic and political imperialism,
aims sometimes pursued in open warfare, as in the Russo-Japanese war,
sometimes by veiled threats, as in the Twenty-one Demands on China.
In the 1930s the undeclared war against China merged with the stated
aim of establishing hegemony in East Asia. The outbreak of war with
the USA in 1941 offered a gambler's chance of extending the bounds
of Japanese rule throughout South-east Asia as well. Since 1945 peaceful economic expansion has been the object and the remarkable
accomplishment of the Japanese government. Recovery, initiated
during the Korean war as part of the USA's defence strategy, proceeded
at an astonishing rate and secured for Japan a premier place throughout
the developed world. This phase of economic expansion has taken
place in the context of a peaceful foreign policy: though by
implication part of the western alliance system, Japan has kept aloof
from the arms race and is constrained by her constitution to do so.
Whether we look at pre- or post-war policies it is important to see
Japan as bound up with the international economy and subject to
its cyclical changes; in the 1930s she became a victim of the great
slump whereas in the 1960s she was able to benefit from the upturn
in world trade.

Japan's military and economic policies, spectacular though they are,
should not deflect our attention from domestic affairs. We need to
recognise and understand the peculiar features in Japanese society
which made it possible for her to undertake such rapid and successful
modernisation. Her social structure provided the seed-bed for the
militant nationalism which flourished before 1945, and the same social
origins may be examined in seeking to explain the resolution with
which recovery was embarked upon thereafter. Although with
American encouragement many of the autocratic features of Japan's
pre-war institutions have given way to more liberal forms of
government, we can see in this state the interesting and instructive
paradox of one of the most highly developed economies in the world
existing in a still largely 'traditional' social structure.

Japan and the World

Nish's scholarly work traces Japanese foreign policy from the beginning of its formative modern period, while Jansen (*Japan and China*) is basic reading for the relations between Japan and China which are in many ways pivotal for the equilibrium of the Pacific basin. Iriye (*After Imperialism*) lays the foundation of the critical decades after the First World War when Japan sought to establish herself as the successor to the western imperial powers in East Asia. Crowley's monograph concentrates on the 1930s when the decisions to invade China and to adopt an autarchic economy were taken. The most dramatic episode of all, the attack on Pearl Harbour, is the central theme of Borg & Okamoto. Jones, on the period of autarchy and war, is authoritative and should be essential reading. Weinstein is very useful for the new peaceful role Japan has assumed in the post-war period.

G.C. Allen	*Japan's Economic Expansion* (Oxford University Press, London, New York, 1965)
M.B. Jansen	*Japan and China: from war to peace 1894-1972* (Rand McNally, Chicago, 1975)
I. Nish	*Japanese Foreign Policy 1860-1942* (Routledge & Kegan Paul, London, Boston, 1977)

* * * *

D. Borg & S. Okamoto (eds.)	*Pearl Harbour as History: Japanese-American relations 1931-1941* (Columbia University Press, New York, 1973)
J.B. Crowley	*Japan's Quest for Autonomy 1930-1938: national security and foreign policy* (Princeton University Press, Princeton, 1966 / Oxford University Press, London, 1967)
D.C. Hellman	*Japan and East Asia: the new international order* (Pall Mall, London, 1972 / Praeger, New York, 1972)

A. Iriye	*After Imperialism: the search for a new order in the Far East 1921-1931* (Harvard University Press, Cambridge, Mass., 1965 / Oxford University Press, London, 1966)
A. Iriye	*Across the Pacific: an inner history of American-East Asian relations* (Harcourt Brace, New York, 1967)
F.C. Jones	*Japan's New Order in East Asia: its rise and fall 1937-1945* (Oxford University Press, London, New York, 1954)

* * * *

D.J. Dallin	*Soviet Russia and the Far East* (Archon Books, Hamden, Conn., 1971, reprint of 1948 edn)
E.R. May & J.C. Thomson (eds.)	*American-East Asian Relations: a survey* (Harvard University Press, Cambridge, Mass., 1972)
A. Ulam	*Expansion and Co-existence: Soviet foreign policy 1917-1973* (Praeger, New York, 2nd edn, 1974)
H.M. Vinacke	*History of the Far East in Modern Times* (Appleton-Century-Crofts, New York, 6th edn, 1959 / Allen & Unwin, London, 1960)
M.E. Weinstein	*Japan's Post-war Defence Policy 1947-1968* (Columbia University Press, New York, 1971)

Japan – the Domestic Perspective

Of the introductory works, Beasley (*Modern History*) gives a balanced survey, and Storry (*History*) provides many insights into Japanese history since the Meiji restoration. Because economic expansion has played such a significant part in Japan's development in the twentieth century, it will be necessary to read some economic history. Allen's book is admirable for imparting information and understanding. Though it emphasises the links between the domestic and the international economies, it does not ignore the social basis on which Japan's economic position rests. Lockwood (*Economic Development*) gives a detailed analysis of economic development in the modern era, taking it up to the eve of war in 1938 while Huh pursues the thread of economic expansion up to the 1960s. An interesting corrective to the praise usually accorded to Japan's economic success is to be found in Halliday & McCormack who see it as a form of aggressive imperialism. In seeking to identify the elements which have enabled Japan to modernise so rapidly, Marshall looks at the special role of the business elite and its contribution to national development. Nakane has written a first-rate brief introduction to the distinctive features of Japanese social organisation. The essays in Dore cover a number of strands in the theme of social change, and the important studies by Havens, Smith and especially Smethurst all focus on the fundamental role of the peasantry. Moore, also concerned with the place of peasants in an autocratic state, cites Japan as one of his main examples. Storry's classic (*Double Patriots*) on militant nationalism is essential reading which can be supplemented by studying the excellent compilation of documents in de Bary. Scalapino and Scalapino & Masumi look at political institutions before and since the war and assess the changes that have taken place in them. Finally, students should note the authoritative volumes which have emerged from a series of conferences on Japanese modernisation. Dore has already been mentioned above. The others are Jansen (*Changing Japanese Attitudes*), Lockwood (*The State*), Ward and Morley.

G.C. Allen   *A Short Economic History of Japan 1867-1937; with a supplementary chapter on economic recovery and expansion 1945-1970* (Praeger, New York, 2nd edn, 1963 / Allen & Unwin, London, 3rd edn, 1972)

W.G. Beasley   *The Modern History of Japan* (Weidenfeld & Nicolson, London, 1963 / Praeger, New York, 1963)

H. Borton   *Japan's Modern Century from Perry to 1970* (Ronald Press, New York, 2nd edn, 1970)

C. Nakane   *Japanese Society* (University of California Press, Berkeley, 1970 / Penguin Books, Harmondsworth, 1973)

R.S. Storry   *A History of Modern Japan* (Penguin Books, Harmondsworth, 1960)

* * * *

W.G. Beasley (ed.)   *Modern Japan: aspects of history, literature and society* (Allen & Unwin, London, 1975 / University of California Press, Berkeley, 1975)

D.M. Brown   *Nationalism is Japan: an introductory historical analysis* (University of California Press, Berkeley, 1955)

R.P. Dore (ed.)   *Aspects of Social Change in Modern Japan* (Princeton University Press, Princeton, 1967 / Oxford University Press, London, 1968)

N. Ike   *Japan: the New Superstate* (W.H. Freeman, Reading, 1974 / Scribner, New York, 1974)

M.B. Jansen (ed.)   *Changing Japanese Attitudes Toward Modernization* (Princeton University Press, Princeton, 1965)

W.W. Lockwood (ed.)   *The State and Economic Enterprise in Modern Japan* (Princeton University Press, Princeton, 1965 / Oxford University Press, London, 1966)

B.K. Marshall   *Capitalism and Nationalism in Prewar Japan: the ideology of the business élite 1868-1941* (Stanford University Press, Stanford, 1967)

J.W. Morley (ed.)   *Dilemmas of Growth in Prewar Japan* (Princeton University Press, Princeton, 1971)

D.H. Shively (ed.)   *Tradition and Modernization in Japanese Culture* (Princeton University Press, Princeton, 1968)

R.J. Smethurst   *A Social Basis for Prewar Japanese Militarism: the army and the rural community* (University of California Press, Berkeley, 1974)

T.C. Smith   *The Agrarian Origins of Modern Japan* (Stanford University Press, Stanford, 1959)

R. Storry   *The Double Patriots: a study of Japanese nationalism* (Chatto & Windus, London, 1957 / Greenwood Press, Westport, Conn., 1973)

R.E. Ward (ed.)   *Political Development in Modern Japan* (Oxford University Press, London, 1968 / Princeton University Press, Princeton, 1968)

* * * *

W.T. de Bary (ed.)   *Sources of Japanese Tradition* (Columbia University Press, New York, London, 1958)

J. Halliday & G. McCormack   *Japanese Imperialism Today: 'Co-prosperity in Greater East Asia'* (Penguin Books, Harmondsworth, 1973 / Monthly Review Press, New York, 1973)

T.R.H. Havens   *Farm and Nation in Modern Japan: agrarian nationalism 1870-1940* (Princeton University Press, Princeton, 1974)

K.-M. Huh   *Japan's Trade in Asia: developments since 1926 – prospects for 1970* (Praeger, New York, 1967)

W.W. Lockwood

The Economic Development of Japan: growth and structural change 1868-1938 (Princeton University Press, Princeton, 1954)

B. Moore

The Social Origins of Dictatorship and Democracy: lord and peasant in the making of the modern world (Penguin Books, Harmondsworth, 1967 / Beacon Press, Boston, 1969)

R.A. Scalapino

Democracy and the Party Movement in Japan: the failure of the first attempt (University of California Press, Berkeley, 1953)

R.A. Scalapino & J. Masumi

Parties and Politics in Contemporary Japan (University of California Press, Berkeley, 1962)

20 SOUTH-EAST ASIA

The idea of South-east Asia as a division of the earth's surface did
not come into being till the creation of South-east Asia Command by
the Allies during the Second World War. The term should not deceive
the historian into imposing upon the area a false unity or sense of
coherence. Culturally it is divided between the Indo-Malay-Polynesian
world primarily of the islands on the southern flank, and the Buddhist-
Confucian areas of the mainland. European colonialism began the task
of building modern states in the area and a point to note is the marked
difference between the styles of British, French and Dutch colonial
government. Nationalist responses, too, varied considerably. In most
states there was a mingling of communist and nationalist organisations
powerfully supported by religious bodies. A question of importance is
why in Indonesia communists were kept subordinate to the nationalist
movement while in Vietnam they captured it. With regard to the timing
of independence from colonial rule, and much else, there is the problem
of the impact of the Japanese occupation of the area in the Second
World War. In the period since independence a key issue is the explanation of the continued failure of the communist movements in Malaysia
and Indonesia as compared with their success in South Vietnam and
the Khmer Republic. This issue also bears in part on the question of
how communist movements win support in peasant societies and in
part on the relations between South-east Asian countries and the outside world.

Hall is the long-standing authority on South-east Asian history, and
Cady offers an extremely detailed treatment of events in the area since
the Second World War. Steinberg provides an excellent analytical introduction, both thematic and sympathetic. Dahm is solid and valuable and
Smith very sensitive. Benda, Von der Mehden and Roff illustrate the
relationship between Islam and nationalism in Indonesia and Malaysia.
Trager provides a slightly dated overview of communist movements in
the area as a whole. McVey and Palmier explain the rise and failure of
the communists in Indonesia, while Duiker explains how they came to
represent nationalism in Vietnam; McAlister is also useful here.
Pluvier's study of the Japanese occupation and decolonisation is
authoritative. Short offers an excellent study of the failure of the
communist insurrection in Malaysia. Of the plethora of works published

on Vietnam, Buttinger has written a monumental narrative history,
Fitzgerald is perceptive about the Americans in the area, Race in an
excellent local study explains how communists won the peasantry
in a district of South Vietnam, and Osborne (*Region of Revolt*) gives
revolt, not only in Vietnam, but also in Malaysia and the Philippines, an
historical perspective. Lyon places South-east Asia in world politics
since 1945.

J.F. Cady	*The History of Post-War Southeast Asia* (Ohio University Press, Athens, 1974)
B. Dahm (tr. P.S. Falla)	*History of Indonesia in the Twentieth Century* (Pall Mall, London, 1971 / Praeger, New York, 1971)
D.G.E. Hall	*A History of South East Asia* (Macmillan, London, 3rd edn, 1968 / St. Martin's Press, New York, 3rd edn, 1968)
J.D. Legge	*Indonesia* (Prentice-Hall, Englewood Cliffs, 1964)
R. Smith	*Vietnam and the West* (Heinemann, London, 1968 / Cornell University Press, Ithaca, 1971)
D.J. Steinberg (ed.)	*In Search of South East Asia: a modern history* (Pall Mall, London, 1971 / Praeger, New York, 1971)

* * * *

H.J. Benda	*The Crescent and the Rising Sun: Indonesian Islam under the Japanese Occupation, 1942-1945* (Van Hoeve, The Hague, 1958)
H.J. Benda	'South-East Asian Islam in the Twentieth Century', in P.M. Holt *et al.* (eds.), *Cambridge History of Islam* vol. II (Cambridge University Press, Cambridge, 1970)

J. Buttinger   *Vietnam: a dragon embattled:* vol. I,
                      From Colonialism to the Vietminh; vol.
                      II, *Vietnam at War* (Pall Mall, London,
                      1967 / Praeger, New York, 1967)

J.F. Cady   *Southeast Asia: its historical development*
                      (McGraw-Hill, New York, 1964)

W.J. Duiker   *The Rise of Nationalism in Vietnam 1900-
                      1941* (Cornell University Press, Ithaca,
                      1976)

F. Fitzgerald   *Fire in the Lake: the Vietnamese and the
                      Americans in Vietnam* (Little, Brown,
                      Boston, 1972)

P.J. Honey   *Genesis of Tragedy: the historical back-
                      ground to the Vietnam War* (Benn, London,
                      1968)

G. McT. Kahin   *Nationalism and Revolution in Indonesia*
                      (Cornell University Press, Ithaca, 1952)

P.H. Lyon   *War and Peace in South-East Asia* (Oxford
                      University Press, London, New York, 1969)

J.M. McAlister   *Vietnam: the origins of revolution* (Allen
                      Lane, London, 1969 / Knopf, New York,
                      1969)

M.E. Osborne   *Region of Revolt: focus on Southeast Asia*
                      (Penguin Books, Harmondsworth, 1971)

L. Palmier   *Communists in Indonesia: power pursued
                      in vain* (Doubleday, New York, 1973)

J.M. Pluvier   *South-East Asia from Colonialism to Inde-
                      pendence* (Oxford University Press, Kuala
                      Lumpur, 1974)

J. Race — *War Comes to Long An: revolutionary conflict in a Vietnamese province* (University of California Press, Berkeley, 1972)

W.R. Roff — *The Origins of Malay Nationalism* (Yale University Press, New Haven, 1967)

A. Short — *The Communist Insurrection in Malaya 1948-1960* (Muller, London, 1975)

S.J. Tambiah — *World Conqueror and World Renouncer: a study of Buddhism and polity in Thailand against a historical background* (Cambridge University Press, Cambridge, 1976)

F.N. Trager (ed.) — *Marxism in South East Asia: a study of four countries* (Stanford University Press, Stanford, 1959)

* * * *

T.A. Agoncillo — *A Short History of the Philippines* (New English Library, London, 1969 / New American Library, New York, 1969)

A. Brackman — *Indonesian Communism* (Praeger, New York, 1963)

O.D. Corpuz — *The Philippines* (Prentice-Hall, Englewood Cliffs, 1965)

D.J. Duncanson — *Government and Revolution in Vietnam* (Oxford University Press, London, New York, 1968)

H.-D. Evers (ed.) — *Modernization in South East Asia* (Oxford University Press, Singapore, 1973)

J.M. Gullick — *Malaysia* (Benn, London, 1969 / Praeger, New York, 1969)

E.J. Hammer	*The Struggle for Indochina, 1940-1955* (Stanford University Press, Stanford, 1966)
P.J. Honey	*Communism in North Vietnam: its role in the Sino-Soviet dispute* (MIT Press, Cambridge, Mass., 1963)
J. Lacouture (tr. P. Wilas)	*Ho Chi Minh: a political biography* (Allen Lane, London, 1968 / Random House, New York, 1968)
J.D. Legge	*Sukarno: a political biography* (Allen Lane, London, 1972)
M. Leifer	*Cambodia: the search for security* (Pall Mall, London, 1967)
J.W. Lewis (ed.)	*Peasant Rebellions in Communist Asia* (Stanford University Press, Stanford, 1974)
R.T. McVey (ed.)	*Indonesia* (Yale University Press, New Haven, 1963)
D.G. Marr	*Vietnamese Anti-Colonialism, 1885-1925* (University of California Press, Berkeley, 1971)
M.E. Osborne	*The French Presence in Cochinchina and Cambodia* (Cornell University Press, Ithaca, 1969)
R. Shaplen	*The Lost Revolution* (Harper & Row, New York, 1965 / Deutsch, London, 1966)
F.R. Von der Mehden	*Religion and Nationalism in Southeast Asia: Burma, Indonesia, the Philippines* (University of Wisconsin Press, Madison, 1963)
D.K. Wyatt	*The Politics of Reform in Thailand: education in the reign of King Chulalongkorn* (Yale University Press, New Haven, 1969)

Britain's Indian empire offers the greatest example of the clash between imperialism and nationalism in the twentieth century. Britain's stake in India was considerable, her impact on Indian society great, her empire the very epitome of imperial rule. The Indian nationalist movement, on the other hand, was notable for the skill with which it was organised and for its distinctive style, producing as it did one of the most remarkable political parties of the century in the Indian National Congress and a charismatic leader in Mahatma Gandhi. The Indian subcontinent also presents two striking examples of successful separatist movements, the first being the Muslim separatist movement which culminated in the foundation of Pakistan in 1947, and the second being the movement for Bangladesh which culminated in the foundation of that state in 1971. Two other major issues since 1947 centre on the problems of Pakistan as a modern state founded on the basis of religion, and the relations between the states of the subcontinent and the great powers in the world beyond.

Wolpert offers the fullest and most up-to-date introduction to the recent history of India. Cohn provides 'feel' for Indian society, Seal outlines the major issues in Indian politics before 1947 and de Bary's collection of readings introduces the major ideas which have influenced Indian thought and action. British imperialism, strange to say, is poorly served by recent research. Nevertheless, Tomlinson's first chapter sets out the declining value of India to Britain in the 1920s and 1930s, while Robb and Moore (see Chapter 4) show how the British devolved power upon the localities while striving to hold on to the essentials at the centre. Indian nationalism, on the other hand, has attracted many historians, and the subject is at the moment dominated by the 'Cambridge school'. Seal (*Emergence*) analyses the social origins and the drives behind the early nationalists. Bayly shows how the Indian National Congress was able to capture power from the British in the localities, Johnson illustrates the way in which the nationalist movement was dominated from time to time by politicians from particular provinces, Brown's two books suggest that Gandhi was as much a politician as a Mahatma, while Baker and Washbrook, among other things, emphasise the relationship between the growth in the range and intensity of government activity and the development of nationalist politics. The background to Muslim nationalism can be found in Hardy. Robinson examines the politics of the separatist movement, while the process of partition is covered by Hodson and Philips & Wainwright. Binder and Rosenthal throw light on the tension between Islam and the modern state in Pakistan, and Jahan and Wilcox explain the emergence of Bangladesh. Burke and Heimsath & Mansingh are useful introductions to the relations between India and Pakistan and the great powers.

W.T. de Bary (ed.)   *The Sources of Indian Tradition* (Columbia University Press, New York, 1958)

B.S. Cohn   *India: the social anthropology of a civilization* (Prentice-Hall, Englewood Cliffs, 1971)

A. Seal   'Imperialism and Nationalism in India', *Modern Asian Studies, 7, 3* (1973)

T.G.P. Spear   *A History of India* vol. II (Penguin Books, Harmondsworth, Baltimore, 1965)

H. Tinker   *South Asia: a short history* (Pall Mall, London, 1966 / Praeger, New York, 1966)

S. Wolpert   *A New History of India* (Oxford University Press, New York, 1977)

* * * *

C.J. Baker   *The Politics of South India 1920-1937* (Cambridge University Press, Cambridge, 1974)

C.A. Bayly   *The Local Roots of Indian Politics: Allahabad 1880-1920* (Clarendon Press, Oxford, 1975)

J.M. Brown   *Gandhi's Rise to Power: Indian politics 1915-1922* (Cambridge University Press, Cambridge, 1972)

| J.M. Brown | *Gandhi and Civil Disobedience: the Mahatma in Indian politics, 1928-1934* (Cambridge University Press, Cambridge, 1977) |

S.M. Burke — *Pakistan's Foreign Policy: an historical analysis* (Oxford University Press, London, 1973)

P. Hardy — *The Muslims of British India* (Cambridge University Press, Cambridge, 1972)

C. Heimsath & S. Mansingh — *A Diplomatic History of Modern India* (Allied Publishers, Bombay, 1971)

H.V. Hodson — *The Great Divide* (Hutchinson, London, 1969)

R. Jahan — *Pakistan: failure in national integration* (Columbia University Press, New York, 1972)

G. Johnson — *Provincial Politics and Indian Nationalism: Bombay and the Indian National Congress 1880-1915* (Cambridge University Press, Cambridge, 1973)

C.H. Philips & D. Wainwright (eds.) — *Partition of India: politics and perspectives 1935-1947* (Allen & Unwin, London, 1970)

F. Robinson — *Separatism among Indian Muslims: the politics of the United Provinces' Muslims 1860-1923* (Cambridge University Press, Cambridge, 1974)

K.B. Sayeed — *Pakistan: the formative phase 1857-1948* (Oxford University Press, London, New York, 2nd edn, 1968)

A. Seal

The Emergence of the Indian Nationalism: competition and collaboration in the later nineteenth century (Cambridge University Press, Cambridge, 1968)

B.R. Tomlinson

The Indian National Congress and the Raj, 1929-1942: the penultimate phase (Macmillan, London, 1976)

D.A. Washbrook

The Emergence of Provincial Politics: the Madras Presidency 1870-1920 (Cambridge University Press, Cambridge, 1976)

W. Wilcox

The Emergence of Bangladesh (American Enterprise Inst. for Public Policy Research, Washington, 1973)

* * * *

S. Arasaratnam

Ceylon (Prentice-Hall, Englewood Cliffs, 1964)

C.J. Baker &
D.A. Washbrook

South India: political institutions and political change, 1880-1940 (Macmillan, Delhi, 1975 / Holmes & Meier, New York, 1976)

W.J. Barnds

India, Pakistan and the Great Powers (Praeger, New York, 1972)

L. Binder

Religion and Politics in Pakistan (University of California Press, Berkeley, 1963)

J.F. Cady

A History of Modern Burma (Cornell University Press, Ithaca, 1958)

M. Edwardes

Nehru: a political biography (Allen Lane, London, 1971 / Praeger, New York, 1972)

J. Gallagher *et al.* (eds.)	*Locality, Province and Nation: essays on Indian politics 1870-1940* (Cambridge University Press, Cambridge, 1973)
D.A. Low (ed.)	*Congress and the Raj: Facets of the Indian struggle 1917-47* (Heinemann, London, 1977)
Z. Masani	*Indira Gandhi: a biography* (Hamish Hamilton, London, 1975 / T.W. Crowall, New York, 1976)
B.N. Pandey	*The Break-up of British India* (Macmillan, London, 1969 / St. Martin's Press, New York, 1969)
C.H. Philips (ed.)	*The Evolution of India and Pakistan: select documents 1853-1947* (Oxford University Press, London, New York, 1962)
E.I. Rosenthal	*Islam in the Modern National State* (Cambridge University Press, Cambridge, 1965)
L.I. & S.H. Rudolph	*The Modernity of Tradition: political development in India* (University of Chicago Press, Chicago, 1967)
K.B. Sayeed	*The Political System of Pakistan* (Houghton Mifflin, Boston, 1967)
K. Siddiqui	*Conflict, Crisis and War in Pakistan* (Macmillan, London, 1972 / Praeger, New York, 1972)
D.E. Smith	*Religion and Politics in Burma* (Princeton University Press, Princeton, 1965)
A. Stein	*India and the Soviet Union: the Nehru era* (University of Chicago Press, Chicago, 1969)

22 WEST ASIA

The break-up of the Ottoman empire during the First World War
signalled the beginning of the transformation of the history of West
Asia. The way was open for the great powers to penetrate to the heart
of the area and the way was also open for the emergence of several new
nationalisms. One major subject is the rise and fall of British, and
to a lesser extent French, influence in the first half of the century.
Points to consider are, first, the nature of British interests in the area and
how they were protected; and second, the impact the British had on
the area and why their power declined. The new nationalisms form a
second major subject. There were nationalisms which embraced a nation,
such as the Turkish, the Iranian and the Egyptian; there was a nationalism which was shared by several states — the Arab; and there were
nationalisms which gained no state at all such as the Armenian and the
Kurdish. Among the many questions which these nationalisms raise are
the relations of some of them with the over-arching Islamic tradition,
and their impact on the politics of the region. Then there is the problem
of Zionism, the most striking nationalism at work in the region but one
imposed from without. It gave birth to the state of Israel the existence of
which has had a continuing and dramatic effect on the politics of the area.
Indeed, the Israeli-Arab conflict which resulted played a part in reducing
British influence, and a considerable part in creating the conditions
in which the USSR and the USA were drawn into the area after the
Second World War. An important theme in the area's relations with
the outside world since 1955 has been the rise and decline of Soviet
influence and the various shifts adopted by the USA to protect her
interests. The chief of these has been, of course, as it has been for
much of the rest of the world, regular supplies of oil.

There is no satisfactory introduction to the full range of problems
presented by West Asia in the twentieth century. Ismael offers an
overview, somewhat jargon-ridden, of the area's relations with the
outside world. Lewis's six lectures (*The Middle East*) are a fine introduction to some major problems, while Mansfield tells the story of
the break-up of the Ottoman empire and its ramifications briefly and
simply. Monroe's treatment of British imperialism in the region is
outstanding. Sachar's vast narrative tomes fill in many details, and
Childers offers the best treatment of the Suez Affair. On Arab

nationalism there are many extremely useful works (Antonius, Zeine, Haim, Hourani, Karpat, Nuseibeh, Binder); Berkes (see Chapter 8), Kushner and Lewis (*The Emergence*) tell the story of Turkey's emergence from the Ottoman empire; Laqueur that of Zionism from the ghettos of eastern Europe; while Upton's brief study remains the soundest introduction to the resurgence of Iran. In approaching Arab-Israeli problems, so often confused by polemic, it is useful to start with documents (Dodd & Sales) and with Allen's general introduction to the issues; Lucas offers a straightforward history of Israel while Abboushi and Rodinson approach matters more from the Arab point of view. Turning to the rise of Soviet influence, Klieman and McLaurin are of an introductory nature, while Lederer & Vucinich and Shamir & Confino provide scholarly and penetrating studies of high standard. The American side is less well served, though Polk is the established authority. On the subject of oil Shwadran looks like replacing Longrigg as the comprehensive treatment. Important aspects of political development are dealt with by Haddad and Bill & Leiden.

T.Y. Ismael	*The Middle East in World Politics: a study in contemporary international relations* (Syracuse University Press, New York, 1974)
B. Lewis	*The Middle East and the West* (Harper & Row, New York, 1966)
P. Mansfield	*The Ottoman Empire and its Successors* (Macmillan, London, 1973 / St. Martin's Press, New York, 1973)

* * * *

R. Allen	*Imperialism and Nationalism in the Fertile Crescent: sources and prospects of the Arab-Israeli conflict* (Oxford University Press, London, New York, 1974)
J.A. Bill & C. Leiden	*The Middle East: politics and power* (Allyn & Bacon, Boston, 1974)
C.H. Dodd & M.E. Sales (eds.)	*Israel and the Arab World* (Routledge & Kegan Paul, London, 1970 / Barnes &

Noble, New York, 1970)

G.M. Haddad   *Revolutions and Military Rule in the Middle East: I The Northern Tier, II The Arab States, III The Arab States Part 2: Egypt, The Sudan, Yemen and Libya* (Robert Speller, New York, 1965-1973)

S. Haim (ed.)   *Arab Nationalism: an anthology* (University of California Press, Berkeley, 1962)

A. Hourani   *Arabic Thought in the Liberal Age, 1798-1939* (Oxford University Press, London, 1962)

K.H. Karpat (ed.)   *Political and Social Thought in the Contemporary Middle East* (Pall Mall, London, 1968 / Praeger, New York, 1968)

W.Z. Laqueur   *A History of Zionism* (Weidenfeld & Nicolson, London, 1972 / Holt, Rinehart & Winston, New York, 1972)

L.J. Lederer &   *The Soviet Union and the Middle East: the post world war II era* (Hoover Inst. Press, Stanford, 1974)
W.S. Vucinich (eds.)

D. Lerner   *The Passing of Traditional Society: modernizing the Middle East* (Free Press, New York, 1958)

P. Mangold   *Superpower Intervention in the Middle East* (St. Martin's Press, New York, 1977 / Croom Helm, London, 1978)

E. Monroe   *Britain's Moment in the Middle East 1914-1956* (Chatto & Windus, London, 1963 / Johns Hopkins Press, Baltimore, 1963)

H.Z. Nuseibeh   *The Ideas of Arab Nationalism* (Cornell University Press, Ithaca, 1956)

W.R. Polk   *The United States and the Arab World* (Harvard University Press, Cambridge, Mass., 3rd edn, 1975)

H.M. Sachar   *The Emergence of the Middle East, 1914-1924* (Knopf, New York, 1969 / Allen Lane, London, 1970)

H.M. Sachar   *Europe Leaves the Middle East 1935-1956* (Knopf, New York, 1972 / Allen Lane, London, 1974)

B. Shwadran   *The Middle East, Oil and the Great Powers* (John Wiley, New York, 3rd edn, 1973)

A. Williams   *Britain and France in the Middle East and North Africa 1914-1967* (Macmillan, London, 1968 / St. Martin's Press, New York, 1968)

* * * *

W.F. Abboushi   *The Angry Arabs* (Westminster Press, Philadelphia, 1974)

M. Abir   *Oil, Power and Politics: conflict in Arabia, the Red Sea and the Gulf* (Cass, London, 1974)

G. Antonius   *The Arab Awakening: the story of the Arab national movement* (Hamish Hamilton, London, 1938 / Garden Press, New York, 1976)

P. Avery   *Modern Iran* (Cambridge University Press, Cambridge, 1965)

L. Binder   *The Ideological Revolution in the Middle East* (John Wiley, New York, 1964)

T.A. Bryson	*American Diplomatic Relations with the Middle East 1784-1975: a survey* (The Scarecrow Press, Metuchan, N.J., 1977)
E.B. Childers	*The Road to Suez: a study of Western-Arab relations* (MacGibbon & Kee, London, 1962)
C.E. Dawn	*From Ottomanism to Arabism: essays on the origins of Arab nationalism* (University of Illinois Press, Urbana, 1973)
J.C. Hurewitz (ed.)	*Soviet-American Rivalry in the Middle East* (Praeger, New York, 1969)
A.W. Kayyali	*Palestine: a modern history* (Croom Helm, London, 1978)
E. Kedourie	*In the Anglo-Arab Labyrinth: the McMahon-Hussayn correspondence and its interpretations 1914-1939* (Cambridge University Press, Cambridge, 1976)
M. Khadduri	*Independent Iraq 1932-1958: a study in Iraq politics* (Oxford University Press, London, New York, 2nd edn, 1960)
M. Khadduri	*Republican Iraq: a study in Iraqi politics since the revolution of 1958* (Oxford University Press, London, New York, 1969)
A.S. Klieman	*Soviet Russia and the Middle East* (Johns Hopkins Press, Baltimore, 1970)
D. Kushner	*The Rise of Turkish Nationalism 1860-1908* (Cass, London, 1977)
J. Lacouture (tr. D. Hofstadter)	*Nasser: a biography* (Secker & Warburg, London, 1973)

W.Z. Laqueur   *The Struggle for the Middle East: the Soviet Union and the Middle East 1958-1968* (Routledge & Kegan Paul, London, 1969)

W.Z. Laqueur   *The Struggle for the Middle East: the Soviet Union in the Mediterranean 1958-1968* (Macmillan, New York, 1969)

B. Lewis   *The Emergence of Modern Turkey* (Oxford University Press, London, New York, 2nd edn, 1961)

T. Little   *Modern Egypt* (Benn, London, 1967 / Praeger, New York, 1967)

S.H. Longrigg   *Oil in the Middle East: its development and discovery* (Oxford University Press, London, New York, 3rd edn, 1968)

N. Lucas   *The Modern History of Israel* (Weidenfeld & Nicolson, London, 1974 / Praeger, New York, 1975)

R.D. McLaurin   *The Middle East in Soviet Policy* (Lexington Books, Lexington, Mass., 1975)

A. Nutting   *Nasser* (Constable, London, 1972 / E.P. Dutton, New York, 1972)

P.R. Odell   *Oil and World Power: background to the oil crisis* (Penguin Books, Harmondsworth, 1974)

M. Rodinson   *Israel and the Arabs* (Penguin Books,
(tr. M. Perl)   Harmondsworth, 1968 / Pantheon Books, New York, 1968)

S. Shamir &   *The U.S.S.R. and the Middle East* (Israel
M. Confino (eds.)   Universities Press, Jerusalem, 1973)

A.L. Tibawi — *The Modern History of Syria, including Lebanon and Palestine* (Macmillan, London, 1969 / St. Martin's Press, New York, 1969)

C. Tugendhat & A. Hamilton — *Oil, the Biggest Business* (Eyre Methuen, London, rev. edn, 1975)

J.M. Upton — *The History of Modern Iran: an interpretation* (Harvard University Press, Cambridge, Mass., 1970)

P.J. Vatikiotis — *Politics and the Military in Jordan: a study of the Arab Legion 1921-1957* (Cass, London, 1967)

Z.N. Zeine — *The Emergence of Arab Nationalism: with a background study of Arab-Turkish relations in the Near East* (Khayats, Beirut, rev. edn, 1966)

23 AFRICA

Though it is difficult to generalise about this huge continent, several strands emerge which are common to nearly all parts of Africa. Imperial rule created the states which achieved (or have yet to achieve) independence: no boundary has been changed and the economies are largely inherited from the former occupying powers. How easy has it been to foster a sense of national identity among disparate elements in traditional and newly modernised societies? What are the remedies for the pervasive conditions of poverty and underdevelopment? Massive aid from outside might speed modernisation yet induce grave social tensions; while rural economies not only find it difficult to survive in the harsh realities of international trade but may also fail to satisfy the aspirations of evolving classes and interests. Both the patterns of government and the endemic instability of successor regimes demand attention; so also do the explosive tensions that lend themselves to ideological pressures from the super-powers who have found Africa a convenient area in which to play out their own rivalries. The new states have tried to mask their differences through the Organization of African Unity, but this has never concealed the many conflicts of interest and policy which separate its members.

Because of its size and complexity few scholars have ventured to generalise about the whole continent, most preferring to rely on case studies of particular states or areas to illustrate their themes. There is no really satisfactory work dealing with the imperial era. Gann & Duignan, vols. 2 and 4, cover some political and economic aspects which provide material for comparisons between the different imperial powers. Vol. 4 also has chapters on some of the social effects of imperialism. Hailey's magisterial work gives the framework of British imperial government. Wilson is a useful recent work with a wide range and coverage. Suret-Canale expertly accounts for the French territories to the end of the Second World War.

McEwan & Sutcliffe give an excellent introduction to the modern problems of Africa while Lloyd offers a theoretical framework for the processes of social change (taking his illustrations from Nigeria). Fallers takes the theme of social stratification in his essays which include the well-known debate about the peasant status of African cultivators. Hunter emphasises the conflict between modernisation and tradition in the cases he examines.

118

Several books deal with underdevelopment. Kamarck and Myint see industrialisation as the ultimate solution to this problem. Though this is not universally accepted, they are useful for their careful elucidation of the many barriers which prevented the rapid adoption of their remedy. Heeger singles out the politics of independence to explain continuing underdevelopment, but this account should be complemented by Arrighi & Saul who analyse the problem in terms of class and capital. Hance's factual work shows how the many facets of the problem interlock with each other. White is the best book on aid, with clear explanations of economic terms and an illuminating discussion on the different interests of donors and recipients.

Military *coups*, and the role of the military in independent states, are important manifestations of the instability of new polities. None of the many studies of these subjects has achieved a wholly satisfactory analysis. Andreski, a sociologist, attempts a diagnosis based on the difficulties of nation building but he also lays stress on the absence of accepted standards of public morality. First's contribution of several case-studies highlights the unsuccessful efforts, to date, to establish lasting civil order. Gutteridge (*Military in Politics*) notes that the military have not played a revolutionary role and that they lack the political skills necessary for stable regimes. In *Military Regimes* he assesses how well the military have performed in government.

Resistance movements against white regimes are dealt with by Gibson in a descriptive work which makes a useful guide. Fanon's angry rhetoric has become a classic expression of the bitterness, and of the expectations, of the Third World on the eve of independence. Rotberg & Mazrui have compiled a massive volume on post-independence revolts which is invaluable for reference. Ogunsawo, Emerson, Brzezinski and Mayall all deal with great-power rivalry. Nolutshungu concentrates on inter-state relations and Wallerstein examines the attempts to preserve continental unity through the OAU, a theme explored also by Wolfers. Mair and Herskowitz give the perspective of two distinguished anthropologists.

L.H. Gann & P. Duignan *Colonialism in Africa 1870-1960:* vol. 2, *The History and Politics of Colonialism 1914-1960;* vol. 4, *The Economics of Colonialism* (Cambridge University Press, Cambridge, 1970-5)

J. Hatch	*Africa Today and Tomorrow: an outline of basic facts and major problems* (Praeger, New York, 1960 / Dobson, London, 2nd edn, 1965)
P.J.M. McEwan & R.B. Sutcliffe (eds.)	*The Study of Africa* (Methuen, London, 1965)
P.J.M. McEwan & R.B. Sutcliffe (eds.)	*Modern Africa* (T.W. Crowall, New York, 1965)
R. Oliver & A. Atmore	*Africa Since 1800* (Cambridge University Press, Cambridge, 2nd edn, 1967)

* * * *

S. Andreski	*The African Predicament: a study in the pathology of modernization* (M. Joseph, London, 1968 / Atherton Press, New York, 1969)
G. Arrighi & J.S. Saul	*Essays on the Political Economy of Africa* (Monthly Review Press, New York, 1973)
Z.K. Brzezinski (ed.)	*Africa and the Communist World* (Stanford University Press, Stanford, 1962)
R. Emerson	*Africa and United States Policy* (Prentice-Hall, Englewood Cliffs, 1967)
L.A. Fallers	*Inequality: social stratification reconsidered* (University of Chicago Press, Chicago, 1973)
W.F. Gutteridge	*The Military in African Politics* (Methuen, London, 1969)
W.F. Gutteridge	*Military Regimes in Africa* (Methuen, London, 1975 / Barnes & Noble, New York, 1975)
W.A. Hance	*African Economic Development* (Pall Mall,

	London, rev. edn, 1967 / Praeger, New York, rev. edn, 1967)
J. Hatch	*Africa Emergent: Africa's problems since independence* (Secker & Warburg, London, 1974 / Contemporary Books, Chicago, 1974)
G. Hunter	*The New Societies of Tropical Africa: a selective study* (Oxford University Press, London, New York, 1962)
S.P. Huntington	*Political Order in Changing Societies* (Yale University Press, New Haven, 1968)
A.M. Kamarck	*The Economics of African Development* (Praeger, New York, rev. edn, 1971)
P.C. Lloyd	*Africa in Social Change* (Penguin Books, Baltimore, 1967 / Penguin Books, Harmondsworth, 1971)
J. Mayall	*Africa: the Cold War and After* (Elek, London, 1971)
H. Myint	*Economic Theory and the Underdeveloped Countries* (Oxford University Press, London, New York, 1971)
G.C. Nolutshungu	*South Africa in Africa: a study of ideology and foreign policy* (Manchester University Press, 1975 / Holmes & Meier, New York, 1975)
A. Ogunsawo	*China's Policy in Africa 1958-1971* (Cambridge University Press, Cambridge, 1974)
R.I. Rotberg & A.A. Mazrui (eds.)	*Protest and Power in Black Africa* (Oxford University Press, London, New York, 1970)

H. Singer &   *Rich and Poor Countries* (Allen & Unwin,
J. Ansari   London, 1977 / Johns Hopkins Press,
                     Baltimore, 1977)

J. Suret-Canale   *French Colonialism in Tropical Africa*
(tr. T. Gottheiner) (Hurst, London, 1971 / Pica Press, New
                     York, 1971)

V. Turner (ed.)   *Colonialism in Africa 1870-1960:* vol. 3,
                     *Profiles of Change: African society and
                     colonial rule* (Cambridge University Press,
                     Cambridge, 1971), cc. 5, 7, 8, 10 and 11.

I. Wallerstein   *Africa, the Politics of Independence: an
                     interpretation of modern African history*
                     (Vintage Books, New York, 1961)

I. Wallerstein   *Africa, the Politics of Unity: an analysis
                     of a contemporary social movement*
                     (Random House, New York, 1967)

C.E. Welch (ed.)   *Soldier and State in Africa: a comparative
                     analysis of military intervention and
                     political change* (Northwestern University
                     Press, Evanston, 1970)

J. White   *The Politics of Foreign Aid* (Bodley Head,
                     London, 1974)

                     * * * *

F. Fanon   *The Wretched of the Earth* (Grove Press,
(tr. C. Farrington) New York, 1965 / Penguin Books,
                     Harmondsworth, 1967)

R. First   *The Barrel of a Gun: political power and
                     the coup d'état* (Penguin Books,
                     Harmondsworth, 1972)

R. Gibson   *African Liberation Movements: contem-
                     porary struggles against white minority
                     rule* (Oxford University Press, London,

New York, 1972)

Lord Hailey — *An African Survey: a study of problems arising in Africa south of the Sahara* (Oxford University Press, London, New York, rev. edn, 1957)

G.A. Heeger — *The Politics of Underdevelopment* (Macmillan, London, 1974 / St. Martin's Press, New York, 1974)

M.J. Herskowitz — *The Human Factor in Changing Africa* (Routledge & Kegan Paul, London, 1962 / Knopf, New York, 1962)

B.W. Hodder & D.R. Harris (eds.) — *Africa in Transition: geographical essays* (Methuen, London, 1967 / Barnes & Noble, New York, 1967)

T. Hodgkin — *Nationalism in Colonial Africa* (Muller, London, 1956 / New York University Press, New York, 1957)

A. Hutchinson — *China's African Revolution* (Hutchinson, London, 1975)

L. Kuper & M.G. Smith (eds.) — *Pluralism in Africa* (University of California Press, Berkeley, 1969)

J.M. Lee — *African Armies and Civil Order* (Chatto & Windus, London, 1969 / Praeger, New York, 1969)

L. Mair — *The New Africa* (Watts, London, 1967)

A.A. Mazrui — *Violence and Thought: essays on social tension in Africa* (Longman, London, 1966 / Humanities Press, Atlantic Highlands, N.J., 1969)

A.A. Mazrui	*Africa's International Relations: the diplomacy of dependency and change* (Heinemann, London, 1977 / Westview Press, Boulder, Col., 1977)
N.C. Pollock	*Studies in Emerging Africa* (Butterworth, London, 1971 / Rowman & Littlefield, Totowa, N.J., 1971)
R.E. Robinson (ed.)	*Developing the Third World* (Cambridge University Press, Cambridge, 1971)
G.W. Shepherd	*The Politics of African Nationalism: challenge to American policy* (Praeger, New York, 1962)
H. Wilson	*The Imperial Experience in Sub-Saharan Africa since 1870* (University of Minnesota Press, Minneapolis, 1977/ Oxford University Press, Oxford, 1977)
M. Wolfers	*Politics in the Organization of African Unity* (Methuen, London, 1976)

Southern Africa

The predominant theme here is race relations, dealt with in the Republic of South Africa by Carter and Hoagland. Marquand provides an easily accessible history in which race relations predominate. Horwitz's analysis is based on solid economic ground. The abortive black African nationalist movement is sympathetically described by Walshe and the factual account by Kotze takes this subject into the 1970s. Simons concentrates on the failure of the white labour movement to associate itself with radical political solutions which might have alleviated the social and economic inequalities suffered by black workers. The mirror of black nationalism is that of white Afrikanerdom whose long struggle to achieve dominance in the Republic is related in Moodie. Bender' study of Angola is important, and so also is the first-hand account by Mondlane of the causes of the prolonged guerrilla resistance to Portugese rule in Mozambique. Nolutshungu has written a useful and original survey of South Africa's relations with the independent black states to the north.

L. Marquand   *The Peoples and Policies of South Africa*
                            (Oxford University Press, London, New
                            York, 4th edn, 1969)

M. Wilson &   *The Oxford History of South Africa:* vol.
L. Thompson (eds.)   II, *South Africa 1870-1966* (Clarendon
                            Press, Oxford, 1971)

                            * * * *

G.J. Bender   *Angola Under the Portuguese: the myth
                            and the reality* (Heinemann, London,
                            1978)

H. Bley   *South-West Africa Under German Rule*
                            (Heinemann, London, 1971 / North-
                            western University Press, Evanston, 1971)

G. Carter   *The Politics of Inequality: South Africa
                            since 1948* (Thames & Hudson, London,
                            1958 / Praeger, New York, 1958)

J. Hoagland   *South Africa, Civilizations in Conflict*
                            (Allen & Unwin, London, 1973 / Hough-
                            ton Mifflin, Boston, 1973)

R. Horwitz   *The Political Economy of South Africa*
                            (Weidenfeld & Nicolson, London, 1967 /
                            Praeger, New York, 1967)

D.A. Kotze   *African Politics in South Africa 1964-
                            1974: parties and issues* (Hurst, London,
                            1975 / St. Martin's Press, New York, 1975

E. Mondlane   *The Struggle for Mozambique* (Penguin
                            Books, Harmondsworth, Baltimore, 1969)

T.D. Moodie   *The Rise of Afrikanerdom: power, apart-*
                           heid and the Afrikaner civil religion
                           (University of California Press, Berkeley,
                           1975)

G.C. Nolutshungu   *South Africa in Africa: a study of ideo-*
                           logy and foreign policy (Manchester
                           University Press, 1975 / Holmes &
                           Meier, New York, 1975)

J. Robertson   *Liberalism in South Africa 1948-1963*
                           (Oxford University Press, London, New
                           York, 1971)

H.J. & R.E. Simons   *Class and Colour in South Africa 1850-*
                           1950 (Penguin Books, Harmondsworth,
                           1969)

P. Walshe   *The Rise of African Nationalism in South*
                           Africa: the African National Congress
                           1912-1952 (Hurst, London, 1970 /
                           University of California Press, Berkeley,
                           1971)

Central Africa

Gray is essential for an understanding of Rhodesia's political history
and of the divided society which has characterised it. But Arrighi's
insights into the class structure are also illuminating. Bergen's work
on the mining industry in Zambia is scholarly and van Onselen is an
exceptionally interesting and original study of labour in Rhodesian
mines. Gérard-Libois gives an admirable account of Katanga province,
illustrating some of the difficulties of creating a national unit out of
very disparate elements in a state like Zaire, the history of which, up to
independence, is briefly but expertly presented by Slade.

G. Arrighi   *The Political Economy of Rhodesia*
                           (Mouton, The Hague, 1967)

R. Gray   *The Two Nations* (Oxford University

Press, London, New York, 1960)

R. Slade · *The Belgian Congo* (Oxford University Press, London, New York, 1960)

A.J. Wills · *An Introduction to the History of Central Africa* (Oxford University Press, London, New York, 3rd edn, 1973)

* * * *

E.L. Bergen · *Labour, Race and Colonial Rule: the copperbelt from 1924 to independence* (Clarendon Press, Oxford, 1974)

J. Gérard-Libois (tr. R. Young) · *Katanga Secession* (University of Wisconsin Press, Madison, 1966)

R. Lemarchand · *Political Awakening in the Congo: the politics of fragmentation* (University of California Press, Berkeley, 1964)

P. Mason · *The Birth of a Dilemma: the conquest and settlement of Rhodesia* (Oxford University Press, London, New York, 1958)

C. van Onselen · *Chibaro: African mine labour in Southern Rhodesia 1900-1933* (Pluto Press, London, 1976 / International Publications Service, New York, 1976)

A. Roberts · *A History of Zambia* (Heinemann, London, 1976 / Holmes & Meier, New York, 1976)

* * * *

R. Palmer · *Land and Racial Domination in Rhodesia* (Heinemann, London, 1977)

East Africa

Volumes II and II of the *History of East Africa* are indispensable for the politics and some aspects of the economics of imperial rule, and Brett looks with a critical eye at the colonial legacy of underdevelopment. Sorrenson explains the hasty attempt, in the aftermath of the Mau Mau rebellion, to create an African landed middle class as a necessary prelude to political independence. Mangat is good on the Asian community caught between the British and the Africans but playing an important economic role.

V. Harlow, E.M. Chilver & A. Smith (eds.) *History of East Africa,* vol. II (Clarendon Press, Oxford, 1965)

K. Ingham *A History of East Africa* (Longman, London, 3rd edn, 1965 / Praeger, New York, rev. edn, 1965)

D.A. Low & A. Smith (eds.) *History of East Africa,* vol III (Clarendon Press, Oxford, 1976)

* * * *

E.A. Brett *Colonialism and Underdevelopment in East Africa: the politics of economic change 1919-1939* (Heinemann, London, 1973 / Humanities Press, Atlantic Highlands, N.J., 1977)

P.H. Gulliver (ed.) *Tradition and Transition in East Africa* (Routledge & Kegan Paul, London, 1969 / University of California Press, Berkeley, 1969)

J.S. Mangat *A History of the Asians in East Africa c. 1886-1945* (Clarendon Press, Oxford, 1969)

M.P.K. Sorrenson *Land Reform in the Kikuyu Country: a study in government policy* (Oxford University Press, Nairobi, 1967)

R.M.A. van Zwanenburg with A. King *An Economic History of Kenya and Uganda 1800-1970* (Humanities Press, Atlantic Highlands, N.J., 1975 /

West Africa

Ajayi & Crowder, though very uneven, serves as a useful introduction
to the history of the region. Crowder's survey of colonial rule emphasises the disadvantages of the imperial era; commendably it does not
deal exclusively with British territories. Hopkins is indispensable, a
model of scholarly synthesis. The background for the civil war in
Nigeria is covered by Luckham and by Miners, while Jones gives a
history of the Nkrumah regime in Ghana, the first of the new states
of West Africa, the collapse of which is attributed to the failure of Ghanaian
society to transform itself rapidly enough to meet the new conditions
and demands of independence. In Foster & Zolberg, the chapter by
Zolberg on the recent political history of the Ivory Coast, and the last
three chapters of comparison, are valuable.

J.F.A. Ajayi &   *History of West Africa,* vol. II
M. Crowder (eds.)   (Longman, London, 1974 / Columbia
                        University Press, New York, 1974)

A.G. Hopkins   *An Economic History of West Africa*
                        (Longman, London, 3rd edn, 1975 /
                        Columbia University Press, New York,
                        1975)

* * * *

S. Amin (tr. F. McDonagh)   *Neo-colonialism in West Africa* (Penguin
                            Books, Harmondsworth, 1973 / Monthly
                            Review Press, New York, 1975)

J.S. Coleman   *Nigeria, Background to Nationalism*
                        (University of California Press, Berkeley,
                        1958)

M. Crowder   *West Africa under Colonial Rule* (Hutchin-
                        son, London, 1968 / Northwestern
                        University Press, Evanston, 1968)

P. Foster &   *Ghana and the Ivory Coast: perspectives*
A. Zolberg (eds.)   *on modernization* (University of Chicago
                        Press, Chicago, 1971)

T. Jones   *Ghana's First Republic* (Methuen, London,
                            1976 / Barnes & Noble, New York, 1976)

R. Luckham   *The Nigerian Military: a sociological
                            analysis of authority and revolt 1960-
                            1967* (Cambridge University Press,
                            Cambridge, 1971)

N.J. Miners   *The Nigerian Army 1956-1966* (Methuen,
                            London, 1971)

K.W.J. Post   *The New States of West Africa* (Penguin
                            Books, Harmondsworth, 1968)

Most Latin American countries gained independence from their colonial rulers over 150 years ago, yet most countries have still to achieve full economic and political independence. The comparison with the USA which gained gained independence but fifty years earlier and the natural resources of which are probably far fewer is striking. The USA is of course the richest society in the world while Latin America is merely the most advanced of the developing areas. The major problem in Latin American history is to explain why economic growth should have been relatively so limited. Important aspects of this problem are: the significance of the colonial legacy, particularly in terms of economic and social structure; the role of the church initially as a conservative force though increasingly, in recent times, as a radical one; the dominance of the great export trades in many economies and their role in limiting capacity to develop self-sustaining economic growth, the intervention of great powers, most notably the USA, in the internal affairs of Latin American countries and their opposition, on occasion, to regimes aiming to bring about rapid social and political change. Further problems centre on the economic and political impact of the economic depression of the 1930s, the emergence and the limited success of the guerrilla movements of the 1960s, and the nature of Latin American political development – the politics of Latin American states have been marked by violence, revolution and dictatorship, particularly the military variety.

Pendle and Calvert provide very brief introductions to the recent history of Latin America, the Steins stress the continuing influence of economic and social structures developed in colonial times, while Furtado is absolutely essential reading for those who wish to understand the fundamental constraints on Latin American economic development. Frank's influential work is now a classic: it offers a sweeping reinterpretation of Latin American history as an aspect of the worldwide spread of capitalism and argues that a social revolution is both necessary and inevitable. Bemis is the established history of the USA's relations with Latin American countries, but now somewhat dated; Connell-Smith provides a comprehensive survey and the essays in Cotler & Fagan should be noted, dealing as they do with important aspects of external control, the multinationals and the Latin American point of view. Poppino examines Soviet activities in the area, Clissold's collection of documents (*Soviet Relations*) has a useful introduction while Parkinson is succinct and has a good bibliography. Mecham, Landsberger (*The Church and Social Change*) and Turner are all excellent studies of the role of the Church while Guzmán's study of Camillo Torres shows how an application of Christian ethics to Colombian society led one priest to espouse revolution, die as a guerrilla and become a powerful symbol of revolutionary change throughout Latin America. Stokes is a useful introduction to the nature of Latin American politics. Johnson's study (*The Military*) of the military in Latin American society from the nineteenth century is excellent but should be read alongside Potash's monograph on Argentina and Stepan's on Brazil. As regards peasant involvement in politics, Womack's study of Zapata's role in the Mexican revolution is a fine work of narrative history, while Petras & Merino's study of one peasant revolt in Fundo Calipran demonstrates that Chilean peasants have a clear understanding of their own self-interest. The last section below consists primarily of monographs of particular societies. Many are remarkable works of scholarship e.g. Adams on Guatemala and Malloy on Bolivia. Cuba, understandably, has attracted more than her fair share of attention, academic and otherwise. Suarez and Ruiz offer sane introductions to the Revolution, Matthews, a journalist who has known Castro since his Sierra Maestra days, gives a sympathetic view and Thomas surveys at massive length 200 years of Cuban history up to the Missile Crisis of 1962.

P. Calvert	*Latin America: internal conflict and international peace* (Macmillan, London, 1969 / St. Martin's Press, New York, 1969)
C. Furtado (tr. S. Macedo)	*Economic Development of Latin America: historical background and contemporary problems* (Cambridge University Press, Cambridge, 2nd edn, 1976)
G. Pendle	*A History of Latin America* (Penguin Books, Harmondsworth, 1967 / Penguin Books, Baltimore, 1969)
S. & B. Stein	*The Colonial Heritage of Latin America: essays on economic dependence in perspective* (Oxford University Press, New York, 1970)

* * * *

R.J. Alexander — *Communism in Latin America* (Rutgers University Press, New Brunswick, 1957)

S.F. Bemis — *The Latin American Policy of the United States: an historical interpretation* (Harcourt Brace, New York, 1943)

S. Clissold — *Latin America: a cultural outline* (Hutchinson, London, 1965 / Harper & Row, New York, 1966)

S. Clissold — *Soviet Relations with Latin America 1918-1968; a documentary survey* (Oxford University Press, London, New York, 1970)

G. Connell-Smith — *The Inter-American System* (Oxford University Press, London, New York, 1966)

J. Cotler & R.R. Fagan — *Latin America and the United States: the changing political realities* (Stanford University Press, Stanford, 1974)

A.G. Frank — *Capitalism and Underdevelopment in Latin America: historical studies of Chile and Brazil* (Monthly Review Press, New York, rev. edn, 1969)

W. Glade — *The Latin American Economies: a study of their institutional evolution* (American Book Co., New York, 1969)

J.J. Johnson — *Political Change in Latin America: the emergence of the middle sectors* (Stanford University Press, Stanford, 1958)

J.J. Johnson — *The Military and Society in Latin America* (Stanford University Press, Stanford, 1964)

H.A. Landsberger (ed.)   *Latin American Peasant Movements* (Cornell University Press, Ithaca, 1969)

H.A. Landsberger (ed.)   *The Church and Social Change in Latin America* (University of Notre Dame Press, Notre Dame, 1970)

J.L. Mecham   *Church and State in Latin America: a history of politico-ecclesiastical relations* (University of North Carolina Press, Chapel Hill, rev edn, 1966)

F. Parkinson   *Latin America, the Cold War and the World Powers 1945-1973: a study in diplomatic history* (Sage, London, Beverly Hills, 1974)

A. Pearse   *The Latin American Peasant* (Cass, London, 1975)

J.F. Petras   *Politics and Social Structure in Latin America* (Monthly Review Press, New York, 1970)

F.B. Pike   *The Conflict between Church and State in Latin America* (Knopf, New York, 1964)

F.B. Pike (ed.)   *Latin American History: select problems: identity, integration and nationhood* (Knopf, New York, 1969)

R.E. Poppino   *International Communism in Latin America: a history of the movement 1917-1963* (Free Press of Glencoe, New York, 1964)

W.S. Stokes   *Latin American Politics* (Thomas Y. Crowell, New York, 1959)

F.C. Turner   *Catholicism and Political Development in Latin America* (University of North Carolina Press, Chapel Hill, 1971)

C. Veliz   *Obstacles to Change in Latin America* (Oxford University Press, London, New York, 1965)

* * * *

R.N. Adams   *Crucifixion by Power: essays on Guatemalan national social structure* (University of Texas Press, Austin, 1970)

J.R. Barager (ed.)   *Why Peron Came to Power: the background to Peronism in Argentina* (Knopf, New York, 1968)

F. Bourricaud   *Power and Society in Contemporary Peru* (tr. P. Stevenson)   (Faber, London, 1970 / Praeger, New York, 1970)

H.F. Cline   *Mexico, Revolution to Evolution 1940-1960* (Oxford University Press, London, New York, 1962)

C.C. Cumberland   *Mexico, the Struggle for Modernity* (Oxford University Press, New York, 1968)

G. Guzmán Campos   *Camillo Torres* (Sheed & Ward, New York, (tr. J.D. Ring)   1969)

K.S. Karol   *Guerillas in Power: the course of the* (tr. A. Pomerans)   *Cuban revolution* (Hill & Wang, New York, 1970 / Cape, London, 1971)

J.M. Malloy   *Bolivia, the Uncompleted Revolution* (University of Pittsburgh Press, Pittsburgh, 1970)

H.L. Matthews   *Castro: a Political Biography* (Allen Lane, London, 1969)

                       Fidel Castro (Simon Schuster, New York, 1969)

J. Petras &
H.Z. Merino
Peasants in Revolt: a Chilean case study 1965-1971 (University of Texas Press, Austin, 1972)

R.A. Potash
The Army and Politics in Argentina (Stanford University Press, Stanford, 1969)

R.E. Ruiz
Cuba: the making of a revolution (University of Massachusetts Press, Amherst, 1968)

T.E. Skidmore
Politics in Brazil, 1930-44: an experiment in democracy (Oxford University Press, New York, 1967)

A. Stepan
The Military in Politics: changing patterns in Brazil (Princeton University Press, Princeton, 1971)

A. Suarez
(tr. J. Carmichael &
E. Halperin)
Cuba: Castroism and Communism 1959-1966 (MIT Press, Cambridge, Mass., 1967)

H. Thomas
Cuba: or the pursuit of freedom (Eyre & Spottiswoode, London, 1971 / Harper & Row, New York, 1971)

J. Womack
Zapata and the Mexican Revolution (Knopf, New York, 1968 / Penguin Books, Harmondsworth, 1972)

25 THE USA IN THE WORLD

In some ways the twentieth century *is* the century of the USA in the world. Emerging for the first time as a world power after the Spanish-American war, the USA took a leading role in the last stages of the First World War and the peace, though its retreat into isolation thereafter implied a certain unreadiness to assume fully the responsibilities that go with world status. The Grand Alliance with Russia in 1941 and the plans for the post-war world signalised the maturity of the USA as one of the super-powers, and as the dominant economic force. The suspicions and misunderstandings which bedevilled its relations with the USSR and resulted in the Cold War formed the main preoccupation in the world arena after 1945. A new concept of its national interests came to dominate American foreign policy, in stark contrast to the isolationism of the inter-war years. This new thinking implied that there were no limits to be set to American national interests and in following this course the USA considered itself obliged to intervene either directly or indirectly in every part of the globe save only Eastern Europe, recognised as the preserve of the USSR, and China after 1949. This intervention took the form of limited wars, ideological struggles and economic imperialism, all seen as part of the strategy to preserve or further American interests and to contain the threat of communism.

Adler and Ambrose between them cover the twentieth century in outline, and Rees is the basic textbook on the Cold War period. Sherwin is very good on the break-up of the Grand Alliance, while Alperowitz is essential reading on the origins of the Cold War. Other detailed studies are to be found in Feis, an official view, and in Horowitz and LaFeber, both critical. Yergin is especially valuable for placing the origins of the Cold War in context, and it also looks at the way in which the development of new thinking about national interests was influenced by various departmental and economic interests. Other assessments of national defence may be studied in Ekirch and Huntington. Osgood and Williams are both important and critical assessments of American foreign policy. The two collections of essays by Chomsky, a philosopher who describes himself as a liberal anarchist, contain some biting and stimulating criticisms of American foreign policy. Particular areas and episodes in it may be referred to in detail in the several titles listed below.

S. Adler

The Uncertain Giant 1921-1941: American foreign policy between the wars (Macmillan, London, New York, 1965)

S.E. Ambrose

Rise to Globalism: American foreign policy 1938-1975 (Penguin Books, Baltimore, rev. edn, 1976)

T.A. Bailey

A Diplomatic History of the American People (Prentice-Hall, Englewood Cliffs, 9th edn, 1974)

A. Rappaport

A History of American Diplomacy (Macmillan, New York, 1975)

D.B. Rees

The Age of Containment: the cold war 1945-1965 (Macmillan, London, 1967 / St. Martin's Press, New York, 1967)

* * * *

E. Abel

The Missiles of October: the story of the Cuban missile crisis (MacGibbon & Kee, London, 1966 / Lippincott, Philadelphia, 1966)

G. Alperowitz

Atomic Diplomacy: Hiroshima and Potsdam; the use of the atomic bomb and the American confrontation with Soviet power (Simon, Schuster, New York, 1965 / Secker & Warburg, London, 1966)

N. Chomsky

American Power and the New Mandarins (Penguin Books, Harmondsworth, New York, 1969)

N. Chomsky

For Reasons of State (Fontana/Collins, London, 1973 / Random House, New York, 1973)

T. Draper

Abuse of Power: U.S. foreign policy from Cuba to Vietnam (Viking Press, New

York, 1967 / Penguin Books, Harmondsworth, 1969)

F.R. Dulles

America's Rise to World Power 1898-1954 (Harper & Row, New York, 1954 / Hamish Hamilton, London, 1965)

A.A. Ekirch

Ideas, Ideals and American Diplomacy: a history of their growth and interaction (Appleton-Century-Crofts, New York, 1966)

H. Feis

From Trust to Terror: the onset of the cold war 1945-1950 (Blond, London, 1970 / Norton, New York, 1970)

D.F. Fleming

The Cold War and its Origins 1917-1960 (Allen & Unwin, London, 1961 / Doubleday, New York, 1961)

D.F. Fleming

America's Role in Asia (Funk & Wagnalls, New York, 1969)

A. Fontaine
(tr. R. Bruce)

History of the Cold War 2 vols. (Pantheon Books, New York, 1968-1969 / Secker & Warburg, London, 1968-1970)

D. Green

The Containment of Latin America: a history of the myths and realities of the good neighbour policy (Quadrangle Books, Chicago, 1971)

E.J. Hammer

The Struggle for Indo-China 1940-1955 (Stanford University Press, Stanford, 1966)

R. Hellmann
(tr. P. Ruof)

The Challenge to US Dominance of the International Corporation (Dunellen, New York, 1971)

D. Horowitz   *From Yalta to Vietnam: American*
                               foreign policy in the cold war (Penguin
                               Books, Harmondsworth, rev. edn, 1969)

D. Horowitz (ed.)   *Containment and Revolution: western*
                               policy towards social revolution, 1917
                               to Vietnam (Blond, London, 1967 /
                               Beacon Press, Boston, 1967)

S.P. Huntington   *The Common Defense: strategic programs*
                               in national politics (Columbia University
                               Press, New York, 1961)

G.McT. Kahin &   *The US in Vietnam* (Dial Press, New
J.W. Lewis   York, 1969)

S. Klebanoff   *Middle East Oil and US Foreign Policy:*
                               with special reference to the US energy
                               crisis (Pall Mall, London, 1974 / Praeger,
                               New York, 1974)

W. LaFeber   *America in the Cold War: twenty years of*
                               revolutions and response 1945-1967
                               (John Wiley, New York, 1969)

W. LaFeber   *America, Russia and the Cold War 1945-*
                               1971 (John Wiley, New York, 3rd edn,
                               1976)

W. LaFeber (ed.)   *The Origins of the Cold War: a historical*
                               problem with interpretations and docu-
                               ments (John Wiley, New York, 1971)

G. Lenczowski   *Russia and the West in Iran 1918-1948: a*
                               study in big power rivalry (Greenwood,
                               New York, 1968)

R.E. Osgood   *NATO, the Entangling Alliance* (Univer-
                               sity of Chicago Press, Chicago, 1962)

R.E. Osgood   *Ideals and Self-interest in American*
                               Foreign Policy: the great transformation

of the twentieth century (University of Chicago Press, Chicago, 1969)

H.M. Pachter — *Collision Course: the Cuban missile crisis and coexistence* (Pall Mall, London, 1963 / Praeger, New York, 1963)

W.R. Polk — *The United States and the Arab World* (Harvard University Press, Cambridge, Mass., rev. edn, 1969)

D. Rees — *Korea, the Limited War* (Penguin Books, Baltimore, 1970)

W.W. Rostow — *The United States in the World Arena: an essay in recent history* (Harper Bros., New York, 1960)

M. Sherwin — *A World Destroyed: the atomic bomb and the Grand Alliance* (Knopf, New York, 1975)

W.A. Williams — *The Tragedy of American Diplomacy* (Dell Publishing Co., New York, 2nd edn, 1972)

D. Yergin — *Shattered Peace: the origins of the cold war and the national security state 1945-1947* (Houghton Mifflin, New York, 1977 / Deutsch, London, 1978)

* * * *

R.J. Barnet — *Intervention and Revolution: the United States in the Third World* (World Publishing Co., New York, 1968)

R.J. Barnet — *Roots of War* (Atheneum, New York, 1972)

D. Borg & S. Okamoto — *Pearl Harbour as History: Japanese-American relations 1931-1941* (Columbia University Press, New York, 1973)

P. Calvocoressi   *World Politics Since 1945* (Longman, Harlow, 2nd edn, 1971

J. Cotler & R. Fagan   *Latin America and the United States: the changing political realities* (Stanford University Press, Stanford, 1974)

C.V. Crabb   *American Foreign Policy in the Nuclear Age* (Harper & Row, New York, 3rd edn, 1972)

R.A. Dahl   *Congress and Foreign Policy* (Norton, New York, 1964)

J.F. Dulles   *War or Peace* (Harrap, London, 1950 / Macmillan, New York, 1950)

R. Emerson   *Africa and United States Policy* (Prentice-Hall, Englewood Cliffs, 1967)

F. Fitzgerald   *Fire in the Lake: the Vietnamese and the Americans in Vietnam* (Little, Brown, Boston, 1972)

L.C. Gardner   *Economic Aspects of New Deal Diplomacy* (University of Wisconsin Press, Madison, 1964)

K. Gough & R. Sharma (eds.)   *Imperialism and Revolution in South Asia* (Monthly Review Press, New York, 1973)

L.J. Halle   *The Cold War as History* (Harper & Row, New York, 1971)

G.S. Harris   *Troubled Alliance: Turkish-American problems in historical perspective 1945-1971* (American Enterprise Inst. for Public Policy Research, Washington, 1972)

A. Iriye   *Across the Pacific: an inner history of*

	American-East Asian relations (Harcourt Brace, New York, 1967)
L.D. Langley	*Cuban Policy of the United States: a brief history* (John Wiley, New York, 1968)
R. MacFarquhar (ed.)	*Sino-American Relations 1949-1971* (Praeger, New York, 1972)
E.R. May	*'Lessons' of the Past: the use and misuse of history in American foreign policy* (Oxford University Press, New York, 1973)
E.R. May & N. Thomson	*American-East Asian Relations: a survey* (Harvard University Press, Cambridge, Mass., 1969)
J. Mayall	*Africa: the Cold War and After* (Elek, London, 1971)
R.E. Neustadt	*Alliance Politics* (Columbia University Press, New York, 1970)
R.E. Osgood	*Alliances and American Foreign Policy: a historical problem with interpretations and documents* (Johns Hopkins Press, Baltimore, 1968)
F. Parkinson	*Latin America, the Cold War and the World Powers 1945-1973: a study in diplomatic history* (Sage, London, Beverly Hills, 1974)
A. Rappaport	*The Big Two: Soviet-American perceptions of foreign policy* (Pegasus, New York, 1971)
E.O. Reischauer	*The United States and Japan* (Harvard University Press, Cambridge, Mass., 3rd edn, 1965)

E.O. Reischauer

Beyond Vietnam: the United States and Asia (Knopf, New York, 1967)

N. Safran

The United States and Israel (Harvard University Press, Cambridge, Mass., 1963)

R.F. Smith

The United States and Cuba: business and diplomacy, 1917-1960 (Bookman Associates, New York, 1961)

J.W. Spanier

American Foreign Policy Since World War II (Praeger, New York, 3rd edn, 1968)

W.A. Williams

The United States, Cuba and Castro: an essay on the dynamics of revolution and the dissolution of empire (Monthly Review Press, New York, 1962)

26 THE USSR IN THE WORLD

The USSR was feared in 1917 for ideological reasons, not for the strength it could wield. Not until the Nazi-Soviet pact was its role as a great power acknowledged. The subsequent formation of the Grand Alliance in 1941 with the western allies confirmed this status and paved the way for Russia's post-war role as the second super-power. The USSR has since that time pursued its foreign policy primarily in defence of its frontiers, especially in Eastern Europe, and secondly as a necessary counterweight in different parts of the world to American intervention. The acquisition of client states, strategic bases and political influence have featured in this phase of activity. Perhaps the most dramatic confrontation with the USA was staged in Cuba in 1962; an attempt to overstep the shadowy bounds set by the USA to the sphere of influence allowed to the USSR. In some respects, however, the most important development in recent decades has been the collapse of the notion that all communist states would follow the Soviet model. The Sino-Soviet split, the most significant manifestation of this change, has had momentous consequences for the triangular relationship between the USA, the USSR and China, and signalled the emergence of a third super-power in world affairs.

Soviet foreign policy in the inter-war years is best followed through the International in Borkenau. Among several general works about Soviet foreign policy, Ulam is scholarly and essential. Dallin is well worth reading because, though limited in time, it was based on Soviet sources. Shulman is useful on Stalin's foreign policy, the cracks in the communist monolith which became so much more obvious after his death are discussed in Brzezinski (*Soviet Bloc*), and the split with China is dealt with in Clubb, North and Lowenthal. Borison & Koloskov represents the official Soviet view. The Cuban crisis may be followed in Pachter, and Soviet strategy more generally in Garthoff, of fundamental importance. Soviet relations with different parts of the world are covered in selected works listed below.

F. Borkenau   *The Communist International* (Faber, London, 1938)

F. Borkenau   *World Communism: a history of the*
                               Communist International (University of
                               Michigan Press, Ann Arbor, 1962)

D.J. Dallin   *The Rise of Russia in Asia* (Archon Books,
                               Hamden, Conn., 1971, reprint of 1948 edn)

P.E. Moseley   *The Kremlin and World Politics: studies*
                               in Soviet policy and action (Vintage Books,
                               New York, 1960)

D.B. Rees   *The Age of Containment: the cold war*
                               1945-1965 (Macmillan, London, 1967 /
                               St. Martin's Press, New York, 1967)

J.F. Triska &   *Soviet Foreign Policy* (Collier-Macmillan,
D.D. Finley   London, 1968 / Macmillan, New York,
                               1968)

A. Ulam   *Expansion and Coexistence: Soviet foreign*
                               policy 1917-1973 (Praeger, New York, 2nd
                               edn, 1974)

                               * * * *

Z.K. Brzezinski   *The Soviet Bloc, Unity and Conflict*
                               (Harvard University Press, Cambridge,
                               Mass., rev. edn, 1967)

Z.K. Brzezinski   *Ideology and Power in Soviet Politics*
                               (Praeger, New York, rev. edn, 1967)

S. Clissold   *Soviet Relations with Latin America*
                               1918-1968: a documentary survey
                               (Oxford University Press, London, New
                               York, 1970)

O.E. Clubb   *China and Russia: the 'Great Game'*
                               (Columbia University Press, New York,
                               1971)

H.D. Cohn   *Soviet Policy Toward Black Africa: the*

	focus on national integration (Praeger, New York, 1972)
H.S. Dinerstein	*Fifty Years of Soviet Foreign Policy* (Johns Hopkins Press, Baltimore, 1968)
R.L. Garthoff	*Soviet Strategy in the Nuclear Age* (Praeger, New York, rev. edn, 1962)
P.J. Honey	*Communism in North Vietnam: its role in the Sino-Soviet dispute* (MIT Press, Cambridge, Mass., 1963)
J.C. Hurewitz (ed.)	*Soviet-American Rivalry in the Middle East* (Praeger, New York, 1969)
R.E. Kanet (ed.)	*The Soviet Union and the Developing Nations* (Johns Hopkins Press, Baltimore, 1974)
W.Z. Laqueur	*The Struggle for the Middle East: the Soviet Union and the Middle East 1958-1968* (Routledge & Kegan Paul, London, 1969)
W.Z. Laqueur	*The Struggle for the Middle East: the Soviet Union in the Mediterranean 1958-1968* (Macmillan, New York, 1969)
W.Z. Laqueur	*Confrontation: the Middle East [war] and world politics* (Wildwood House, London, 1974 / Quadrangle/New York Times Book Co., New York, 1974)
R.D. McLaurin	*The Middle East in Soviet Policy* (Lexington Books, Lexington, Mass., 1975)
R.C. North	*Moscow and Chinese Communists* (Stanford University Press, Stanford, 1953)

R.E. Poppino   *International Communism in Latin America: a history of the movement 1917-1963* (Free Press, New York, 1964)

M.D. Shulman   *Stalin's Foreign Policy Reappraised* (Harvard University Press, Cambridge, Mass., 1963)

I. Spector   *The Soviet Union and the Muslim World 1917-1958* (University of Washington Press, Seattle, 1959)

A. Stein   *India and the Soviet Union: the Nehru era* (Chicago University Press, Chicago, 1969)

                        * * * *

O.B. Borisov &   *Soviet-Chinese Relations 1945-1970*
R.T. Koloskov   (Indiana University Press, Bloomington,
(tr. V. Petrov)   1975)

G.S. Harris   *The Origins of Communism in Turkey* (Hoover Inst. Press, Stanford, 1967)

G.F. Kennan   *Russia and the West under Lenin and Stalin* (Hutchinson, London, 1961)

A.S. Klieman   *Soviet Russia and the Middle East* (Johns Hopkins Press, Baltimore, 1970)

W. LaFeber   *America, Russia and the Cold War 1945-1975* (John Wiley, New York, 3rd edn, 1976)

G. Lenczowski   *Soviet Advances in the Middle East* (American Enterprise Inst. for Public Policy Research, Washington, 1972)

R. Lowenthal   *World Communism: the disintegration of a secular faith* (Oxford University Press, New York, 1964)

J. Mayall	*Africa: the Cold War and After* (Elek, London, 1971)
H.M. Pachter	*Collision Course: the Cuban missile crisis and coexistence* (Pall Mall, London, 1963 / Praeger, New York, 1963)
B. Shwadran	*The Middle East, Oil and the Great Powers* (John Wiley, New York, 3rd edn, 1974)
F.N. Trager (ed.)	*Marxism in South East Asia: a study of four countries* (Stanford University Press, Stanford, 1959)
T.W. Wolfe	*Soviet Power and Europe 1945-1970* (Johns Hopkins Press, Baltimore, 1970)
D. Yergin	*Shattered Peace: the origins of the cold war and the security state* (Houghton Mifflin, New York, 1977 / Deutsch, London, 1978)
S. Zabih	*The Communist Movement in Iran* (University of California Press, Berkeley, 1966)

The nineteenth-century tradition of balanced alliance systems was destroyed in the First World War; the peacemaking was governed by the fact of the Bolshevik Revolution and the strenuous efforts made by the USA to counteract the its danger to a free enterprise economy in the rest of the world. The League of Nations was intended to be a central feature of this western international order but in the event it failed to avert the anarchy of the inter-war years. Only the grave dangers of war pushed the USA and the USSR into suspending their hostility, the formation of the Grand Alliance in 1941 heralding the tardy assumption by these two great powers of their rank as arbiters of the world. But this marriage scarcely survived the war: misunderstandings, miscalculations and deliberate challenges in the immediate post-war era and, above all, the threat of nuclear force by the USA, made real diplomacy between the super-powers increasingly difficult. The creation of an international organisation in 1945 was intended more to reassure the public than itself to assume responsibility for the balance of world power, but the flaws inherent in the United Nations prevented it from adequately performing this function. Its work has thus been hampered by great-power rivalry, by power blocs, by regional interests, and, not least, by the sovereign independence of member states. But it should be said that, political differences notwithstanding, the underlying trend of the later twentieth century has been towards greater economic unity and interdependence.

Though difficult to read, the two books by Mayer are well worth the trouble: they look beyond the facade of diplomacy and reveal the motives and pressures behind policy making. Fleming is basic, a classic account of the way in which relations between the USA and the USSR were determined from 1917. This argument is also followed by Yergin who has much to say about the institutionalisation of American interests in and after the Second World War. Walters remains the unrivalled exposition of the structure and work of the League of Nations. Rees, a basic textbook, accounts for the onset of the Cold War on which Alperowitz makes essential reading. Feis presents the State Department view of that period, Horowitz and LaFeber are revisionists; so also is Fontaine, though his analysis is weaker at the end. The structure of the UN is explained by the businesslike Nicholas,

Higgins looking at its work more generally, and James and Burns at its
role as a peacekeeping body. Nuclear politics are the theme of Quester
while Richards explains international economic institutions. Not many
works deal with the Russian side which makes D.J. Dallin, based on
Russian sources, especially valuable. Garthoff is another basic work
on Russian policy.

P. Calvocoressi   *World Politics Since 1945* (Longman,
                         Harlow, 2nd edn, 1971)

D.F. Fleming   *The Cold War and its Origins 1917-1960*
                         (Allen & Unwin, London, 1961 / Double-
                         day, New York, 1961)

D.B. Rees   *The Age of Containment: the cold war
                         1945-1965* (Macmillan, London, 1967 /
                         St. Martin's Press, New York, 1967)

D. Yergin   *Shattered Peace: the origins of the cold
                         war and the national security state*
                         (Houghton Mifflin, New York, 1977 /
                         Deutsch, London, 1978)

                         * * * *

G. Alperowitz   *Atomic Diplomacy: Hiroshima and Pots-
                         dam; the use of the atomic bomb and the
                         American confrontation with Soviet
                         power* (Simon, Schuster, New York,
                         1965 / Secker & Warburg, London, 1966)

D.W. Bowett   *The Search for Peace* (Routledge & Kegan
                         Paul, London, Boston, 1972)

A. Dallin (ed.)   *The Soviet Union and Disarmament: an
                         appraisal of Soviet attitudes and intentions*
                         (Praeger, New York, 1964)

H. Feis   *From Trust to Terror: the onset of the
                         Cold War 1945-1950* (Blond, London,
                         1970 / Norton, New York, 1970)

R.N. Gardner	*In Pursuit of World Order: U.S. foreign policy and international organizations* (Praeger, New York, rev. edn, 1966)
J. Gittings	*The World and China 1922-1972* (Methuen, London, 1974 / Harper & Row, New York, 1975)
R. Higgins	*United Nations Peacekeeping 1946-1967: documents and commentary* 2 vols. (Oxford University Press, London, New York, 1969-1970)
D. Horowitz	*From Yalta to Vietnam: American foreign policy in the cold war* (Penguin Books, Harmondsworth, rev. edn, 1969)
A. James	*The Politics of Peacekeeping* (Chatto & Windus, London, 1969 / Praeger, New York, 1969)
M. Mark	*Beyond Sovereignty* (Public Affairs Press, Washington, 1965)
L.W. Martin	*Arms and Strategy: an international survey of modern defence* (Weidenfeld & Nicolson, London, 1973)
A.J. Mayer	*Politics and Diplomacy of Peacemaking: containment and counterrevolution at Versailles, 1918-1919* (Weidenfeld & Nicolson, London, 1968 / Vintage Books, New York, 1969)
A.J. Mayer	*Political Origins of the New Diplomacy 1917-1918* (Vintage Books, New York, 1970)
H.G. Nicholas	*The United Nations as a Political Institution* (Oxford University Press, London, New York, 5th edn, 1975)

G.H. Quester

Nuclear Diplomacy: the first twenty-five years (Dunellen, New York, 1970)

H. Seton-Watson

Neither War nor Peace: the struggle for power in the post-war world (Methuen, London, 1960 / Praeger, New York, 1966)

A. Ulam

Expansion and Coexistence: Soviet foreign policy 1917-1973 (Praeger, New York, 2nd edn, 1974)

F.P. Walters

A History of the League of Nations (Oxford University Press, London, New York, 1960)

* * * *

A.K.H. Boyd

Fifteen Men on a Powder Keg: a history of the Security Council (Methuen, London, 1971 / Stein & Day, New York, 1971)

H. Bull

The Anarchical Society: a study of order in world politics (Macmillan, London, 1977 / Columbia University Press, New York, 1977)

A.L. Burns &
N. Heathcote

Peace-keeping by U.N. Forces from Suez to the Congo (Pall Mall, London, 1963 / Praeger, New York, 1963)

D.J. Dallin

The Rise of Russia in Asia (Archon Books, Hamden, Conn., 1971, reprint of 1948 edn)

A. Dulles

The Secret Surrender (Harper & Row, New York, 1966)

A. Fontaine
(tr. D.D. Paige)

History of the Cold War: vol. I, *From the October Revolution to the Korean War, 1917-1950*; vol.II, *From the Korean War to the Present* (Secker & Warburg, London, 1968-70 / Pantheon Books, New York, 1968-9)

R. Garthoff

Soviet Strategy in the Nuclear Age
(Praeger, New York, rev. edn, 1962)

J.M. Jones

The United Nations at Work (Pergamon,
New York, Oxford, 1965)

W. LaFeber

*America, Russia and the Cold War 1945-
1975* (John Wiley, New York, 3rd edn,
1976)

E. Luard (ed.)

The Evolution of International Institutions
(Thames & Hudson, London, 1966 /
Praeger, New York, 1966)

E. Luard (ed.)

*The International Regulation of Frontier
Disputes* (Thames & Hudson, London,
1970 / International Publications Service,
New York, 1970)

J. Newhouse

Cold Dawn: the story of SALT (Holt,
Rinehart & Winston, New York, 1973)

G.H. Quester

The Politics of Nuclear Proliferation
(Johns Hopkins Press, Baltimore, 1974)

J.H. Richards

International Economic Institutions
(Holt, Rinehart & Winston, London, New
York, 1970)